REPENTANCE FROM SIN

How Antinomianism Disarmed the Gospel and Not the Sinner

By

Joshua Joscelyn

Truth & Mercy Baptist Publications
Milton, FL

ISBN-10: 0692855017
ISBN-13: 978-0692855010

Library of Congress Control Number: 2017903223

Cover art by Daniel Valles

Join the community: Facebook.com/repentancefromsin

Published by Truth & Mercy Baptist Publications
Milton, FL

Printed in the United States of America

To my dear friend, Jason,
who I am convinced will
come to the acknowledging of
the truth in God's good time.

TABLE OF CONTENTS

PROLOGUE

From the dawn of time, man has existed in a state of rebellion against Almighty God. History is littered with the casualties of this bitter war, and there is no sign of it ever abating.

God's first act towards man, His beloved creation, was to put him in a perfect garden with all the good gifts he could ever want. He gave him good food, fitting fellowship, and dominion over God's creation. Man could walk hand-in-hand with God in beautiful harmony and fellowship, glorifying God in His holiness, benevolence, and infinite goodness. But how did man repay his infinitely good God? How long did his loyalty last before he slipped his hand out of the hand of the Creator and with it grasped a dagger? At the first opportunity, man, who had more reason to adore and worship God than any other creature ever created, plunged the knife into the hand of his God, essentially biting the hand that fed him.

In turn, God sent His prophets to plead with His lost creation, to restore humanity to fellowship and goodness. Time after time, emissaries from the Kingdom of Heaven stood up in the public square and wept for the bloody treason that was being committed en masse against the one Holy God who loved them more than they could have loved themselves. But because they loved themselves more than they loved God, they stoned those emissaries of reconciliation sent to warn them of the error of their ways. Again, the dagger came down, plunged into the back of God's messengers.

And so Almighty God – so infinitely holy, so incomprehensibly powerful and terrible – responded yet again. Though He could have ended it once and for all and squashed the pitiful insurrection, He chose to show his unfathomable love in the person of His Son, who stepped down from the throne of heaven and came down to the world of men to offer Himself as payment for the treason that ravaged the whole race. Here man was given the ultimate opportunity to see the boundless love of Almighty God. An outstretched hand reached down from heaven to reconcile the sinner to God. And mankind did the only thing he knew how to do. The dagger fell yet again, and Christ was brutally butchered by the sin-ravaged blackguards of this world.

One day, God's mercy will rest. He will come with a swift and terrible vengeance and execute His holy wrath on the race of men. There will be no emissaries. There will be no pleading with man. There will be no mercy. There will be only silence – as the last rebel is cast into hell for all eternity. God will be glorified in the execution of the traitorous race. But that day is not yet here. Peace does not yet reign.

Sadly, those very people who think to escape the inevitable end of the war against God believe they can do so while clinging to their weapons of war against the Savior.

Today the war still rages, and every person alive has a choice. Which side will they join? Everyone is born into the ranks of the rebellion, but not everyone must die a rebel's death. While the majority of humankind is actively engaged in treason with every resource available to them, creating evil inventions and tools of war, God is still calling individuals to His side. He still extends a hand of forgiveness and full pardon. The blood of Jesus has satisfied the wrath of God for all those who will apply it. From time to time, in every corner of the earth, sinners can be seen abandoning their posts in the rebellion and fleeing across the battlegrounds into the arms of a Savior who still loves them and still wants them to escape the coming final judgment.

But not everyone who says, "Lord, Lord," will enter into His rest. Many of those who come to Him still have a secret they hope to conceal along the road to heaven. Old habits die hard, and many of the supposed defectors carry with them the telltale dagger of sin. They foolishly think they can pull one over on God. This time He will not notice. This time will be different. But will it? Sadly, those very people who think to escape the inevitable end of the war against God believe they can do so while clinging to their weapons of war against the Savior. What a surprise they will find when they get to the gate and find no pardon available to them.

INTRODUCTION

An ancient lie is once again brewing in modern Christianity. Once cast down as a false gospel many generations ago, this lie is regaining and surpassing its former popularity in our churches. But it is subtle. It is not readily identifiable on its face as the heretical lie it truly is. In fact, it masquerades as the true gospel of faith alone and speaks out against preaching of the law and holiness, calling such preaching *legalism* or a works-based gospel. Repentance from sin is quietly removed from the message, and in its place is inserted a disarmed and powerless gospel that does not change sinners into saints or remove the dagger of sin from the clutches of sinful rebels. A simple repeat-after-me prayer is typically all that separates the child of wrath in the world from the child of wrath in the pew. Indeed, the devil's children walk and talk among us. They have been let in the back door on an empty profession of faith. No surrender needed.

Many well-meaning Christians are caught up in the deception and fall for this lie that repentance only means to turn from unbelief to belief. They do not understand that saving faith involves a change of direction. They believe that – at least on this earth – God's children can bear some resemblance to the world. And many of them have come to accept a lack of victory over sin and the presence of rank wickedness in the houses of God as unavoidable or even acceptable. On the other hand, there are some who simply find this cheap gospel all too convenient for their carnal, part-time Christianity. They prefer an easy belief that costs them nothing. And so they nod along when someone claims the sinner's prayer saves souls and when the preacher claims sin is no big deal, since it was paid for at Calvary.

In recent generations, the gospel has been disarmed by a shift from holiness preaching to an empty sales pitch that allows the sinner to keep his sin. Repentance from sin has been done away with, and in its place an easy-belief system now assures sinners they are on their way to heaven. And so it should come as no surprise that most converts fall away within a matter of months or that the morality in the pew varies precious little from that in the world. The issue of sin was not dealt with in their lives, and so no transformation or new birth truly changed them.

Sadly, this is no new lie, but a repurposed old heresy resurrected to deceive new generations. Martin Luther first encountered it when he soundly refuted the sect of the Antinomians in the early 1500s. Stemming from a disregard for God's law and holiness, this old error has once again made gradual headway among churchgoers and is now common among those we know and love. So many do not realize the sinister nature of this subtle modification of the gospel. So few understand that it fails to disarm the sinner and instead renders the gospel powerless to truly save souls from both hell and their sin.

A Gate to Hell

In the parable by John Bunyan, *The Pilgrim's Progress*, the dreamer tells of seeing Christian enter the Celestial City after crossing the river of death. It is a glorious time when faith is made sight. Christian and those who traveled life's road in his footsteps finally arrive at the wondrous gates of heaven and prepare to meet their Savior. Christian presents his certificate and is invited in to receive his reward. This is the joy hoped for by everyone who names the name of Christ. But another pilgrim, named Ignorance, also crosses over and, because he has no such certificate, meets with a tragic and terrifying surprise:

> When he was come up to the gate, he looked up to the
> writing that was above, and then began to knock, supposing

that entrance should have been quickly administered to him. But he was asked by the men that looked over the top of that gate – Whence come you, and what would have? He answered – I have eat and drunk in the presence of the King, and He has taught in our streets. Then they asked him for his certificate, that they might go in and show it to the King. So he fumbled in his bosom for one, and found none. Then said they – Have you none? But the man answered never a word. So they told the King; but He would not come down to see him, but commanded the two Shining Ones that conducted Christian and Hopeful to the city, to go out and take Ignorance, and bind him hand and foot, and have him away. Then they took him up, and carried him through the air, to the door that I saw in the side of the hill, and put him in there. Then I saw that there was a way to hell even from the gate of heaven...[1]

Today's churchgoers are in for a terrifying surprise. Many – perhaps most – will find one day that there is a way to hell even from the church pew. When the Lord judges the quick and the dead, many of the respected members and leaders of the conservative, fundamentalist churches of America will

"Then I saw that there was a way to hell even from the gate of heaven."

be horrified to learn this fact firsthand. And why? It is simple, really. For the same reason Ignorance was cast into hell when he thought he would be welcomed into heaven. Because they entered not at the strait gate. They did not have the right gospel. Jesus explained about this proper gate in Matthew 7:

Enter ye in at the strait gate: for wide is the gate, and broad is the way, that leadeth to destruction, and many there be which go in thereat: Because strait is the gate, and narrow is the way, which leadeth unto life, and few there be that find it.[2]

Many will probably read this and think to themselves that this must be referring to those liberals who add works to the gospel or who preach obviously false gospels as the cults do. Yet this book will prove that there is a false gospel being preached in conservative, evangelical churches – even in fundamentalist Baptist churches and churches who claim to hold firmly to the fundamental doctrines of the Bible in the face of rampant apostasy and compromise. It is in these churches and circles that an insidious false gospel has arisen resulting in a frightening phenomenon: these churches are full of lost people.

This book will uncover just what this false gospel is, where it is often found, what it sounds like, what its fruit is, and just how to respond to it biblically. It is an ancient heresy, but it has only been revived on a large scale in the past few generations. Its message is diabolical and ever more so for the fact that it sounds so much like the true gospel. Its adherents are friends, family, and fellow church members. It can go undiscovered for years, and it is damnable and spreading even among good churches and good people of God. It must be exposed, rooted out, and stopped.

Tares Among Wheat

In the Gospel of Matthew, Christ relates a parable of the tares. He tells of a man who sowed a field of good wheat but noticed something strange when the seeds germinated and sprang up. Many of the plants were actually tares – weeds – not good wheat. This would not do. After all, wheat would bring forth good fruit, profitable for the nourishment of many. But tares would be worthless and of no value to anyone. When his helpers came to him about the problem, the householder replied that, because the young wheat and tares were almost indistinguishable, they would have to be separated at harvest time, and not before – and that the tares would be burned in the end. He furthermore left no doubt in their mind who was responsible for this tragic infiltration. It was not happenstance – "An enemy hath done this."[3]

Think about the sinister nature of this situation. This parable was intended to warn of the fact that there will be children of the devil walking among saints, talking among saints, ministering among saints. And ultimately, their true identity will not be revealed until the very end – at "the manifestation of the sons of God," as Paul puts it in Romans.[4] At times, but not always, some might blow their cover, as it were, and leave the congregation of the redeemed in a clear display of their damnable pedigree. John the apostle writes about this in I John:

> They went out from us, but they were not of us; for if they had been of us, they would no doubt have continued with us: but they went out, that they might be made manifest that they were not all of us.[5]

Appropriately, the great reformer, Martin Luther, warned about this very phenomenon in his *First Disputation Against the Antinomians,* fearing the rise of an unregenerate generation in the pews of God's Church – a disguised, alien generation inserted into our midst by the very machinations of Satan himself. Luther warned in no uncertain terms:

> ...that we by no means permit an alien and new way of teaching the article of justification – especially during our lifetime – to be taught, lest by our negligence we provide an occasion for Satan to burst into the Church and to give rise to endless sects and offenses. We must not only be concerned about how we might be saved, but we also must take the greatest pains lest posterity receive lies and errors under the disguise of piety and truth. Yet let those be accursed who are, or will be, the authors of such horrible evil.[6]

In folklore, the ancients feared something they called a *changling.* It was often said that leaving a baby unattended might result in a fairy or troll snatching it away and installing in its place their own infant. The inattentive mother would raise the babe as her own, not realizing the child she suckled was not necessarily hers or even human. The underlying fear of the old wives' tale was that this child might one day remember where he came from in the night or at some inopportune time. He might answer the call of his devious ancestry. Who knows what dangers might lurk in their own home if their own child were not what he appeared to be?

This silly superstition may well have been unfounded, yet it should not be ignored. For Christ tells His followers to be watchful and judge righteous judgment for a very similar reason. What if children of the devil are in our own homes, walking and talking among us like brothers? Christians should be able to tell men by their fruits and discern whether or not they be true sons of God or tares among wheat. If they entered not at the strait gate of repentance and faith, they are not saved, and they will be unfruitful. Their lives will not be characterized by victory over sin, zeal for righteousness, or love of the brethren. Oh, they will put on a good show, and they may even seem to be great soul winners or ministry leaders. But the telltale signs of an imposter will be present, visible to those who take the time to contrast them with the Bible.

Humanism in the Church

How did the western church come to such a place? What brought about this sinister infiltration? In the powerful sermon, *Ten Shekels and a Shirt*, Paris Reidhead describes the rise of *fundamentalism* in the early 1900s. The great missionary, teacher, and author points out that

Salvation has been reduced to a get-out-of-hell-free card won merely by agreeing with the fundamentals of the faith.

the average church members in America believe in the death, burial, and resurrection of Christ. They believe all the fundamentals of the faith. And yet they are dead, weak, and unsaved. How did this happen? In the early 1900s, many conservative Christians sought to distinguish themselves from the theological liberalism that had swept over the world in the previous century. They banded together under a manifesto of fundamental beliefs they all held in common and agreed that they believed in these things because they were fundamentalists. But the next generation came along, according to Reidhead, and agreed that they were fundamentalists because they believed in these things.[7] This subtle reversal is the very essence of the change that took place in the western Church.

And so, today, if someone can give mental assent to a formula of doctrines, he is pronounced a Christian and enrolled in the local church. The sinner is now told only that he must pray a prayer and mentally agree to certain things, so he will not have to go to hell. Perhaps it is not as simple as that in some circles, and yet even there it is primarily an intellectual or emotional affair. Salvation has been reduced to a get-out-of-hell-free card won merely by agreeing with the fundamentals of the faith. Yet the Bible teaches that salvation is the act of reconciliation between a filthy sinner and a holy God, and that it is marked by a changed life. It is a supernatural and transformative act of God.

This imposter gospel, this seditious and subverting philosophy, has a name: *humanism*. Reidhead points out that the aim of humanism is the happiness of man. And on this criterion, there is no difference between theological liberalism and fundamentalism. "The liberal says the end of religion is to make man happy while he's alive," Reidhead points out. Yet "the fundamentalist says the end of religion is to make man happy when he dies."[8] They are both the same in their causes and effects. And when this debate over the law and the gospel is boiled down to its base parts, make no mistake, the issue is whether or not man is saved for God or whether man is saved for himself. Whereas the Bible teaches that sin is the ultimate problem solved by the gospel, the Antinomian will say the ultimate problem solved by the gospel is hell. One sees the problem through God's eyes, the other through man's. And this, as Reidhead concludes, "is the betrayal of the ages."

Antinomianism in the Modern Era

This work will endeavor to prove that lost men sit in fundamentalist pews today because they have been told that repentance is not necessary for salvation, and that this seemingly new heresy is in reality descended from the ancient cult of the

Whereas the Bible teaches that sin is the ultimate problem solved by the gospel, the Antinomian will say the ultimate problem solved by the gospel is hell.

Antinomians that opposed Martin Luther 500 years ago. And for this reason, it is not coincidental that those who remove repentance from the gospel tend to lead carnal lives as a general rule. In fact, it is to be expected, because Antinomianism means "anti-law" or "lawlessness." And this desire to remove repentance from the gospel is the logical outgrowth of an unhealthy apathy towards sin and is often indicative of unregenerated souls, unconvicted of the depravity of their own sin.

The correlation between a carnal lifestyle and an aversion to preaching the gospel of repentance is nowhere more evident than in the case of the apparent godfather of the modern antinomian movement: Jack Hyles. Hyles rose to prominence among fundamentalists in the 1960s as a pastor, traveling evangelist, and author. He redefined repentance to no longer mean that which it had always been understood to mean in a biblical context: a turning of the heart and mind away from sin. He began telling people that it only meant turning from unbelief to belief.[9] Freed from the restrictions of plowing up the ground of the sinner's heart to prepare it for conviction, repentance, and faith, Hyles now could tell sinners to just turn from their unbelief and say the sinner's prayer – and they would be saved (and he would not be in violation of all the scriptures that spoke about repentance being necessary for salvation). The result? His church, First Baptist

Church of Hammond, swelled dramatically, eventually reaching a membership of 100,000 people.[10]

But as for the spiritual state of the church, it has since come to light that Jack Hyles, his extended family, his ministerial staff, and many of the church members were engaged in rampant immorality, including adultery, homosexuality, child molestation, wife swapping, and more.[11] Why were these iniquities allowed to continue unchecked? Why did First Baptist of Hammond not confront and end these escapades? Why did Hyles not respond to solid evidence of these sins when it was presented to him? Why did he and his staff merely cover up these scandals? Why did he, himself, lead the pack in the number and depravity of these sins? Why? Because he was an Antinomian – a lawless one. His theology was tailor made for lost men to feel safe and secure in their sinful rebellion against God. No need to put your dagger down; God will give you heaven with or without it. No need to repent of your sins and surrender to the Almighty; you are going to heaven anyway. Just keep those sins, say this little prayer, eat, drink, and be merry. This false gospel and carnal immorality go hand in hand.

No, not everyone who rejects the role of repentance from sin in the gospel is a lost sex fiend. Not everyone who redefines repentance to mean turning from unbelief is necessarily living in sin. In fact, Antinomians typically believe they are fighting for the cause of salvation by grace through faith, as though repentance is some new works-based gospel. They typically do not even know their doctrine makes them Antinomians. Many of them are upstanding people who simply believe they are fighting against legalism. Yet there is an undeniable correlation between lawless living and a gospel that does not deal with the issue of sin. And more often than not, the Antinomian who tosses repentance out of the gospel will at the very least excuse his sin as a normal part of being human or as not that big of a deal. He will languish in spiritual ineffectiveness and defeat, always seeking to do better, but never being that bothered when he fails. And this is to be expected. It is the logical end of such a heretical twisting of the gospel of Jesus Christ. And what is more, it is not new.

A Lie Resurrected

The modern evangelical hatred for repentance in the gospel is no new evil. It is the old lie of Satan first termed *Antinomianism* in the early 16th century by Martin Luther in his valiant defense of the proper role of conviction, law, and repentance in the gospel. This old lie has simply been repackaged. Today, those who claim the gospel does not include repentance merely echo the unbiblical lies first refuted by Luther hundreds of years ago. And, though they often claim to be only interested in upholding faith alone for the glory of God, a false gospel that leaves men

The lie of Antinomianism willonlyperpetuate the war against God on a covert scale, giving the sinner boldness in his sin rather than a new heart.

stumbling in their rebellion does not, and never will, glorify God. An antinomian plan of salvation will never bring a man to drop his dagger, put up his white flag, and surrender to the will of God. The lie of Antinomianism will only perpetuate the war against God on a covert scale, giving the sinner boldness in his sin rather than a new heart.

For too long this deceptive and destructive philosophy has plagued our churches and our gospel. A thorough and sound refutation of this lie in all its aspects is long overdue. It is time to bury this wicked lie and embrace the true gospel that changes lives. It is time to restore repentance to its rightful place in the gospel.

Chapter 1

ANTINOMIANISM

Behold, ye trust in lying words, that cannot profit. Will ye steal, murder, and commit adultery, and swear false-ly, and burn incense unto Baal, and walk after other gods whom ye know not; And come and stand before me in this house, which is called by my name, and say, We are delivered to do all these abominations?
Jeremiah 7:8-10

What is Antinomianism? Where did it start? How does it differ from the true gospel? Isn't this just a semantical issue? Is this such a significant issue, or is it just splitting hairs? Whenever one enters into a discussion or debate regarding the role of repentance in the gospel, it is tempting to conclude that this is only a small disagreement or perhaps even a matter only of semantics. On one hand there are those who say repenting from sin is a work and thus requiring it in the plan of salvation is adding works to the gospel. On the other hand, there are those who say without repentance you cannot be saved. Surely this disagreement with our own brothers is a small one. Surely the disagreement could not truly be this stark when it revolves around the most fundamental doctrine in the Bible: the gospel, itself. Could it?

Disregarding the Law

Unfortunately, the divide is much deeper than most people realize before deep study or frequent exposure to the controversy.

This heresy stems from a complete misunderstanding of the purpose of the gospel and a total devaluation of God's holy law.

And it goes back to a group of long-refuted heretics in the 16th century known as the Antinomians or "lawless ones." Today, the antinomian heresy has descended to our generation in the form of what is often called *easy believism* or *quick prayerism*, but the underlying philosophy is still the same. If close attention is paid in discussing this matter with those who reject the role of repentance in the gospel, inevitably an underlying theme will grow painfully obvious. This heresy stems from a complete misunderstanding of the purpose of the gospel and a total devaluation of God's holy law. Rather than viewing the gospel as God's method of reconciling lawbreakers, paying the just fine for our crimes, and freeing us from the bondage of sinning against a holy God, the adherents of this error view the gospel as God's method of saving humanity from an unpleasant afterlife in hell. To them, hell is the problem solved by salvation, not sin. And if saints continue sinning after salvation, oh well – at least they are still going to heaven when they die. Rather than placing the emphasis on the transgression of God's law and the affront to a holy God, they place the emphasis on the removal of the punishment. And so, this humanistic philosophy, at its very core, stems from a pervasive disregard for God's law and sees hell as the problem more than the sin.

Does the gospel not save us from hell? Of course! But only as a byproduct, not a prime product. While the Bible does tell us that God's mercy saves us from hell, consider the numerous scriptures that describe salvation as being from sin. For example (emphasis added):

Repent ye therefore, and be converted, **that your sins may be blotted out.**

Acts 3:19

And she shall bring forth a son, and thou shalt call his name Jesus: for he shall save his people **from their sins.**

Matthew 1:21

Who gave himself for us, that he might redeem us **from all iniquity, and purify unto himself** a peculiar people, zealous of good works.

Titus 2:14

Let him know, that he which converteth the sinner from the error of his way shall save a soul from death, **and shall hide a multitude of sins.**

James 5:20

And so we shall confirm that the true nature of this heresy is Antinomianism, a disregard for the importance of, integrity of, and reconciliation with God's law. It has been called by other names, but the name, *Antinomianism*, most accurately identifies the very core of this error. Some have labeled it *easy believism* because it seems to make salvation too easy, reducing it to a mental agreement with a few basic tenets of the faith. However, proponents of this belief system argue that salvation *is* easy, and then point to this label to argue that advocates of repentance are trying to add works to the gospel and make the gospel difficult. Other good Christian authors like David Cloud have sidestepped this accusation by naming it *quick prayerism*, because this camp often claims people can be saved simply by saying a quick, little prayer, as though salvation could be reduced to a short incantation. Either label is fitting, and yet both come up short in some way.

The gospel is simple, albeit not necessarily easy. In fact, Jesus said in Mark, "It is easier for a camel to go through the eye of a needle, than for a rich man to enter into the kingdom of God."[12] For this reason, *easy believism* seems a rather appropriate term for the most part. But on the other hand, Christ also said in Matthew, "my yoke is easy, and my burden is light."[13] So many prefer the term, *quick prayerism.*

However, many of those who reject the role of repentance in the gospel also reject the repeat-after-me method of winning converts. So this label does not fit these people, as they argue that you have to have genuine faith, with or without a simple little prayer, in order to be saved – but that repentance from sin only comes after salvation. So, while neither of these labels are a perfect fit for the various segments of those rejecting repentance, all of these segments hold in common the antinomian perspective of the law. And this undervaluing of the law influences their gospel and cheapens it, either to a quick prayer or to a faith that does not include surrendering to the Lord and putting down their dagger of rebellion. For this reason, *Antinomianism* is the most appropriate term for this false gospel.

The True Gospel

What is the true gospel? For two thousand years, the true Church of Jesus Christ has taught the simple truth that Jesus came into the world to save sinners from the power and penalty of sin. Through repentance toward God, and faith toward our Lord Jesus Christ,[14] who was born of a virgin, lived a sinless life, and died and rose again, damned souls can be redeemed and reborn as new creatures with a new nature that will never pass away. Having put their faith in the atoning blood shed on Calvary to wash their sins from the record books, the saint is eternally secure and will never see damnation. Not by works of righteousness, which are as filthy rags, but by the washing of regeneration man is supernaturally born of God.

The Bible could not be clearer on an issue so central as the very gospel. Repentance and faith are inseparable gifts from God, without which no man can receive the grace that saves. Jesus, Himself, famously said in Luke, "Except ye repent, ye shall all likewise perish."[15] The apostle Paul described this gospel in II Corinthians, "For godly sorrow worketh repentance to salvation not to be repented of."[16] The apostle Peter made it clear that our sins could be washed away through the conversion brought about by repentance.

He said in Acts, "Repent ye therefore, and be converted, that your sins may be blotted out."[17] Even in the Old Testament, God described this regeneration and salvation that could be granted through repentance. Speaking through Ezekiel, He said:

> Cast away from you all your transgressions, whereby ye have transgressed; and make you a new heart and a new spirit: for why will ye die, O house of Israel?[18]

From the beginning, the Church took seriously this great commission from our Savior "that repentance and remission of sins should be preached in his name"[19] and echoed this message in their creeds, statements of faith, and preaching. Far from being an addition of works to the gospel in recent times, the role of repentance in the gospel has always been considered orthodox and commonplace in the churches of Jesus Christ. A brief look at some of the great Baptist and Protestant creeds and statements of faith throughout bygone centuries renders this assertion absolutely undeniable:

Having put their faith in the atoning blood shed on Calvary to wash their sins from the record books, the saint is eternally secure and will never see damnation.

> Unfeigned Repentance, is an inward and true sorrow of heart for Sin, with sincere confession of the same to God, especially that we have offended so gracious a God, and so loving a Father; together with a settled purpose of Heart, and a careful endeavor to leave all our sins and to live a more holy and sanctified Life, according to all God's Commands.
> *Orthodox Baptist Creed of 1679*[20]

This saving repentance is an evangelical grace, whereby a person, being by the Holy Spirit made sensible of the manifold evils of his sin, doth, by faith in Christ, humble himself for it, with godly sorrow, detestation of it, and self-abhorrency; praying for pardon and strength of grace, with a purpose and endeavor by supplies of the Spirit, to walk before God unto all well-pleasing in all things.

Philadelphia Baptist Confession of Faith of 1742[21]

We believe that repentance and faith are sacred duties and also inseparable graces, wrought in our souls by the regenerating Spirit of God; whereby being deeply convinced of our guilt, danger, and helplessness, and of the way of salvation by Christ, we turn to God with unfeigned contrition, confession and supplication for mercy; at the same time heartily receiving the Lord Jesus Christ as our Prophet, Priest and King, and relying on him alone as the only and all-sufficient Saviour (sic).

New Hampshire Confession of Faith of 1833[22]

Repentance is a turning from a life of self and sin to a life of submission and obedience to God's will. Repentance, as used in the New Testament, means a change of mind, but it is a word of moral significance and does not mean merely a change of opinion. Such a change often takes place without repentance in the New Testament sense. The will is necessarily and directly involved, as well as the emotions, but in scriptural repentance there is a change of mind with reference to sin, a sorrow for sin and a turning from sin. Repentance means sins perceived, sins abhorred and sins abandoned. This change is wrought by the power of God through the Holy Spirit, the word of truth being used as a means to convict the sinner of sin and lead

Far from being an addition of works to the gospel in recent times, the role of repentance in the gospel has always been considered orthodox and commonplace in the churches of Jesus Christ.

him to forsake it and to resolve henceforth to walk before
God in all truth and uprightness.

Fundamentals of the Faith, 1922[23]

Contained within the doctrinal statements above, asserting the
role of repentance in the gospel, is also an idea of how repentance
might be defined. In a nutshell, repentance is simply a change of
heart and mind regarding deeds or actions, committed or intended,
that results in a change of course. In the 1828 edition of Webster's
Dictionary, it is defined as such:

> To feel pain, sorrow, or regret for something done or spoken...
> to change the mind in consequence of the inconvenience or
> injury done by past conduct...to sorrow or be pained for sin,
> as a violation of God's holy law, a dishonor to his character
> and government, and the foulest ingratitude to a Being of
> infinite benevolence.[24]

Webster goes on to quote theologians by way of providing
examples of this definition:

> Repentance is a change of mind, or a conversion from sin
> to God.
>
> Hammond
>
> Repentance is the relinquishment of any practice, from
> conviction that it has offended God.
>
> Johnson[25]

The Antinomian Gospel

The Antinomians of recent years have come along and turned
this gospel on its head. No longer are repentance toward God and
faith toward our Lord Jesus Christ considered free grace. Holding
the law of God in such low esteem as they do, they have labeled
repentance a work, thus arguing that simply surrendering to God is too
much effort to put forth to receive the gift of mercy. Like the slothful
man mentioned in Proverbs 26:15, putting their hand to their mouth to

feed themselves would just be too much. There are several different strands of this heresy, but a few common variations and identifying expressions of it include:

- Repentance is not necessary to be saved – it comes after salvation.
- Repentance is necessary, but it just means turning from unbelief, not from sins.
- Unbelief is what damns the sinner, so repentance is only from unbelief.
- Repentance is just a change of mind.
- No one can repent of all sin. No one can even remember all their sins.
- Salvation by repentance is Lordship salvation, and if you cease to make Him Lord, you could lose your salvation.
- God repented more than anyone else in Scripture, so repentance could not mean turning from sin.

Therefore, while some will deny the role of repentance in the gospel outright and tell you to not even use the word in evangelism, others will acknowledge the abundance of scriptures linking repentance with the gospel and conclude that it only means a change of mind about God or about believing in Him. They will often create strawmen arguments to knock down. Confusing confession with repentance, they will say no one can repent of every single sin ever committed. Forgetting that the same would hold true of exercising faith for salvation, they will argue that repenting for salvation would mean the loss of salvation should future sins go unrepented of. Painted this way, it is no wonder repentance sounds bad. But this is not the true gospel, nor are these valid characterizations of or objections against repentance.

While objections to repentance will be dealt with extensively in Chapter 8, let us briefly examine the re-definition of repentance at this time for a more thorough understanding of just how subversive the antinomian gospel is. Possibly the most frustrating thing about discussing the issue of repentance with an Antinomian is how they redefine the simple word, *repent*. Commonly, it is pointed out that the word simply means *to turn*. And that is true. Stripped of all its context and connotation, the word basically means to turn. Yet, when we compare scriptures with scriptures, we find that it more fully means a change of heart and mind regarding actions, committed or intended, virtually every single time it appears in the Bible.

Merely consulting a dictionary would reveal that *turn* also fits this assertion. While the Antinomian is quick to say that repentance simply means to turn, a quick look at Webster's 1828 dictionary reveals the same things about "turn" that the Antinomian hates so much. Among its various definitions, the dictionary tells us the verb means:

> To change or shift sides...to change; to transform... to metamorphose...to change direction to or from any point...to move from a direct course or strait line; to cause to deviate...to reverse...to change a course of life; to repent..."[26]

Obviously, the Antinomian is correct to point out the link between *repent* and *turn,* yet he does not fully realize that he is merely begging the question, simply pushing back the same debate to another word.

Yes, the sinner must repent or "turn" in order to be saved. And no, it is not the turning or repenting that does the saving. Yet, without this change in orientation, the sinner is no candidate for grace. This concept of the turning sinner was explored in greater detail in a brief book by Dr. David Turner, aptly named, *The Turn*. In the introduction, Dr. Turner tells of his observations after a lifetime in ministry observing hundreds of one-on-

Repentance is a change of heart and mind regarding actions, committed or intended, virtually every single time it appears in the Bible.

one conversions that "no one goes from completely wicked one day to saved the next. (Ezek. 18:27)."[27] While he quickly offers up that the new birth is an instantaneous event, Dr. Turner has observed that sinners always go through a change of the mind and heart prior to yielding to the gospel. He adds that there is "a process of time before conversion when the sinner gets sick and tired of his way of life and desires a change."[28]

Yet this change is not always forthcoming or divinely inspired. At times, according to Dr. Turner, the sinner seeks to merely turn over a new leaf only to wind up back in the ditch – something the Bible calls worldly sorrow. But Godly sorrow is not to be repented of. Eventually, the sinner may come to find this permanent repentance, which "begins in the mind and culminates in a turn of the body away from sin."[29] It is this turn that the Bible calls repentance and says must happen in the mind of the sinner before God can supernaturally save them. The turn must happen in the mind and heart before it can happen in the body and life.

A Bait-And-Switch Trick

While the Antinomian might admit that a turn is necessary to be saved, he is reticent to speak of this turn in the context of the gospel. In fact, it is considered wrong technique by many Antinomians to speak to sinners about sin or having to give anything up. In their logic, God will clean up the sinner once he is saved, so why bother talking about sin and repentance before? This is a bait-and-switch gospel that flies in the face of the clear proclamation of Scripture that all men must be saved from their iniquities. It is not meant to be some dark secret that the saint will no longer be able to live in sin. On the contrary, it is part of the gospel we are instructed to proclaim from the rooftops. God does not trick the sinner into giving Him his heart and then rob him of his sin like some common mugger or con man. Instead, as we see in the case of the rich young ruler, Christ lays out the value proposition in no uncertain terms. Take it or leave it.

So why cannot the Antinomian speak about sin and judgment and the law when giving the gospel to a sinner in need of saving? Quite simply because of the cult of love that pervades our degraded society. Nowadays, if someone speaks about sin to a sinner, they are deemed "unloving" and no longer fit to listen to.

This is a bait-and-switch gospel that flies in the face of the clear proclamation of Scripture that all men must be saved from their iniquities.

For whatever reason, if an Antinomian actually finds himself in an evangelistic conversation, he is quick to talk about grace with little to no mention of the sin that makes grace necessary. This way, he remains loving and relevant to the sinner. In his mind, if he can get the sinner to simply pray a little prayer or believe in Jesus really, really hard, then God will save him and begin to work on his sins, even if he knew nothing about this arrangement previously. Rather than risk turning the sinner off to the gospel and to Jesus, the Antinomian talks about heaven and grace with only a token "admit you are a sinner" hastily thrown in under his breath when outlining the sinner's prayer. And as long as the sinner says the prayer and mentally assents to what the presenter tells him about God and the Bible, he is saved, a bona fide born-again, child of God. But he is not. He is still a child of the devil.

Inoculated to the Gospel

By and large, Western culture – especially in the US – has been completely inoculated to the gospel by the watered-down message of unconditional love and acceptance. No longer is the gospel a demand for surrender, but rather an invitation to let some hippie Jesus "love on" the sinner and accept him as he is with all his sins and flaws. Go to any major festival, rock concert, or public gathering, stand on a stool, and preach the judgment of God. You will be amazed how many people will come up to you and tell you they are already saved – with booze in hand, half naked, and swearing at you for being unloving. These blatant sinners can tell you the Romans Road, that God is a loving and forgiving God, and in many cases that they got saved earlier in life – many times describing a seemingly flawless gospel as that which saved them. As it turns out, nearly everyone is "saved."

So why are they partying with a drunken group of godless infidels? Because God is forgiving. He understands their heart. God does not care how you live, as long as you believe in His Son, right? This is especially common in the southern US, the *Bible Belt,* as it has been nicknamed. With a church on every corner and a dozen gospel stations on the radio, the south is full of "Christians" partying the whole way to hell. And because they are confident in their antinomian conversion story that never involved putting anything down or picking up a cross, they have no ears for the true gospel. They want nothing to do with it. It harshes their glory buzz. In other words, they are utterly immune to the true gospel. They have the guilt problem out of the way, and they can still go to church and nod along with the average preacher, so live and let live!

The Bible tells us that God's law is perfect, "converting the soul."[30] Without first plowing up the hard ground of sinfulness, pride, and self-righteousness, the good news of the gospel is worthless to the sinner. God never intended for lost rebels to hear only the good news of the gospel, but for them to first understand their need for this good news. Giving the sinner the information that God is forgiving before convincing – or convicting – them of their sin is dangerous. Emboldened by just enough knowledge of grace and heaven to assume they are forgiven and headed there, they persist in their old ways never having been truly born again.

In his powerful book, *Finding the Reality of God*, the great expositor and missionary, Paris Reidhead, echoes this very problem in the modern Church:

If I had my way, I would declare a moratorium on public preaching of "the plan of salvation" in America for one to two years. Then I would call on everyone who has the use of the airwaves and the pulpits to preach the holiness of God, the righteousness of God and the law of God, until sinners would cry out, "What must we do to be saved?" Then I would take them off in a corner and whisper the Gospel to them. Such drastic action is needed because we have gospel-hardened a generation of sinners by telling them how to be saved before they have any understanding why they need to be saved.[31]

The average person on the street already knows about the love and forgiveness of God. But he needs to hear more about the law and wrath of God if he is to have any chance of truly being regenerated. Rather than trick him into saying a prayer or assenting to a few theological assertions with the intent to get him hooked on Jesus only for Jesus to pounce on his sins when he least expects it, the preacher should lay out the plainness and simplicity of the gospel demand, as Christ and the apostles did. Repent and be converted that your sins may be blotted out! Unless ye repent, ye shall all likewise perish! But instead, we have learned to welcome unregenerate tares into our midst so long as they have had a salvation experience and can nod along with our doctrinal assertions. And we now have changlings and devils sitting in our pews, teaching our Sunday-school classes, and even pastoring our churches.

In what is possibly his greatest sermon, *Ten Shekels and a Shirt*, Paris Reidhead concluded this very thing from having observed and participated in the fundamentalist movement for decades. He lamented the humanistic mindset of the fundamentalist:

And so it wasn't long until it got to our generation where the whole plan of salvation was to give intellectual assent to a few statements of doctrine. And a person was considered a Christian because he could say "Uh huh" at four or five places that he was asked to, and if he knew where to say 'Uh huh,' someone would pat him on the back, shake his hand, smile broadly, and say: "Brother, you're saved."[32]

The great 18th-century commentator, Matthew Henry, warned against those who would prop up the sinner in his sin by giving him a false sense of security in his comments on Ezekiel 13:22. The verse states:

> Because with lies ye have made the heart of the righteous sad, whom I have not made sad; and strengthened the hands of the wicked, that he should not return from his wicked way, by promising him life:

Matthew Henry called out the modern antinomian heresy vividly in adding:

> Those have a great deal to answer for who grieve the spirits, and weaken the hands, of good people, and who gratify the lusts of sinners, and animate them in their opposition to God and religion. Nor can anything strengthen the hands of sinners more than to tell them that they may be saved in their sins without repentance, or that there may be repentance though they do not return from their wicked ways.[33]

"Nor can anything strengthen the hands of sinners more than to tell them that they may be saved in their sins without repentance, or that there may be repentance though they do not return from their wicked ways."

In our humanistic, antinomian society, the gospel is no longer about God's justice being satisfied. It is no longer about a supernatural conviction for sins, a work of the Holy Ghost that transforms an individual from a slave of sin into a servant of holiness. Instead, it is merely an intellectual concession allowing the sinner some freedom from guilt and full admission into the religious ranks for as long as he chooses to live out this delusion. Perhaps God will surprise him and take away his sin after he gets saved. But perhaps not.

A Case Study

I, myself, had the unfortunate opportunity to see this antinomian gospel play out in the life of a false convert in full confirmation of my thesis that removing biblical repentance produces tares among wheat. Several young people in a Bible study I once attended took great issue with repentance in the gospel. One young woman who was there with her newly saved husband explained how my insistence on preaching repentance from sin, even if correct, would turn the sinner off and make him hate God for being a judge over his sin. It would be better to leave off talking about sin until after the sinner were saved, and then let God handle their sin. She went so far as to say that she had no idea she was a sinner until after she was converted, and that, if I had been the one preaching to her, perhaps she might never have been saved. I reluctantly informed her matter-of-factly that she simply could not possibly be born again even now, because Christ only came to save the lost. If a person does not see themselves as a sinner in need of a Savior, how is the gospel relevant to them? How can they possibly be born again?

We parted ways over our strong disagreement. But several years later, after I had begun work on this book, our paths crossed again. I found out this young woman had completely renounced her Christian faith, divorced her husband, and begun living a wicked life of open rebellion against God as a professing atheist. There was no surprise on my part. Years ago, I had told her directly that she was no child of God, but rather an imposter deceived by the antinomian gospel. It was only a matter of time until she showed her true colors. And sadly, she did just that only a few short years after my warning.

So I told her about my book and asked if I could interview her as a lost woman who now openly rejected Christianity but had once sat in the pews of an independent Baptist church as an accepted sister in Christ. She consented to discussing the matter with me for my book, and her words served as a complete confirmation of the problem with this antinomian gospel: it focuses on mental assent to (or belief in) doctrinal statements without dealing with the issue of sin. It posits a manmade formula rather than a divine intervention. Essentially, it leaves the sinner confident and secure in his sin, promising him eternal life without holiness, without which the Bible says no one will see the Lord.[34] As long as the sinner says a prayer or believes really hard, he can keep his dagger of sinful pleasures.

I asked her about her conversion, how she had initially converted, and what had brought about her conversion. Reflecting back, she said:

> I had converted after getting a better understanding of the theology…I started reading and studying the bible afterwards and listening to sermons from a wide variety of Christians.[35]

Her description of her false conversion spoke only of theology and agreeing with what she called "fundamentalist literature." She then discussed the problem she later realized she had with this fundamentalist doctrine – the doctrines of guilt and damnation. She went on to say, "I grew increasingly disturbed by the idea that all humans deserve eternal damnation." And so, having been converted by assenting to mere doctrine of belief in Jesus, she was free to renounce her assent to this doctrine and no longer be a child of God. But through it all, she admitted that God had never fundamentally changed her or dealt with her sin. She stated:

> I latched onto the idea that Jesus loved us all enough to die for us regardless of the level of sin we had committed… my core morality never felt changed.[36]

When asked just what she had thought the point of Calvary was and what she once believed about why Christ died on the cross, she came back with a perfectly humanistic, antinomian response, not mentioning God's justice or the price for sin, but only God's love and desire to spare humanity from hell:

> ...the purpose of the gospel was to show people the love Christ had for people by dying on the cross. He did that so we could escape the suffering in the afterlife/death and live forever in peace near God.[37]

To this woman who had once, as a professing Christian, railed against including repentance from sin in the gospel, the whole point of Calvary was to keep her hide from being singed and to make her happy in the afterlife. It had nothing to do with satisfying the wrath of God or

"I latched onto the idea that Jesus loved us all enough to die for us regardless of the level of sin we had committed... my core morality never felt changed."

paying for her treason against Almighty God. And in her mind, she became a Christian by believing in "fundamentalist literature" that did not change her "core morality" or disarm her in her sinful rebellion. Thus it comes as no surprise that she likewise ceased being a Christian merely by choosing to no longer believe in those things. It is worth reminding the reader at this time that this woman was for some time a regular at the local independent Baptist church. But she proved to be a tare, a false convert among us, thanks to the heresy of Antinomianism.

Chapter 2

THE ANCIENT CONTROVERSY

For there are certain men crept in unawares, who were before of old ordained to this condemnation, ungodly men, turning the grace of our God into lasciviousness, and denying the only Lord God, and our Lord Jesus Christ.

Jude 4

In examining the modern heresy of Antinomianism, which rejects the role of repentance from sin in the gospel, it is important to also understand its roots. The heresy is no new idea, but an ancient one that goes back to the Old Testament. Men have always wanted to feel secure in their sins. They have always wanted to feel that God is not as angry with them and their sin as their conscience tells them. And so the ultra-grace philosophy was born.

In essence, ultra grace is just another title for that philosophy which belittles the commandments – or law – of God and their relevance in our lives. Some pretend that being born again means they are no longer under any obligation to obey God's commands or that sin in the life of the believer is not a matter of significance, since it has been paid for by Christ's sacrifice. While the Bible teaches that a Christian is no longer under the law, the commandments of God are not to be ignored – especially when it comes to soteriology or the doctrine of the gospel. Whether or not the Christian is obligated to the spirit of the moral law, there is no denying the role of God's law in the conviction process that leads to salvation.

The negative attitude towards the law of God and the flippant attitude towards sin that characterizes those who rail against repentance is rooted in a controversy that reared its ugly head in the early 16th century. While its modern heir can certainly be traced primarily to the mega-church pastor, Jack Hyles, and his redefinition of the term, *repentance*, in the latter half of the 20th century, we can ultimately trace it back to the *First Antinomian Controversy* of the early 1500s between the great reformer, Martin Luther, and his protégé, Agricola of Eisleben. And in this monumental controversy, which spanned nearly two decades, the proper gospel was upheld and Agricola's deviation from it refuted. While there are some differences in the Antinomianism of today and that of the 16th century, there is no denying the relation and the many similarities between the modern and ancient varieties.

In the interest of providing an historical framework and demonstrating that this newly prominent heresy has already been refuted by some of the greatest minds of the Protestant Reformation, we shall endeavor to go back in time and explore what happened in the early 1500s. We will uncover what the arguments for this false gospel were back then and how they have been modified for current generations and explore how they and their modern counterparts were discredited long ago. There is nothing new under the sun, and we shall bear out that to discredit the role of repentance from sin in the gospel is not merely to teach easy believism or quick prayerism, but is actually to resurrect the ancient controversy of the Antinomians in all its tired failures and bankruptcy.

The First Antinomian Controversy

In 1525, a young protégé of Martin Luther, Johannes Agricola published his first printed work, a commentary on the Gospel of Luke. The book introduced several ideas that would soon become the crux of a great controversy. In it, Agricola argued that the law was only

To discredit the role of repentance from sin in the gospel is not merely to teach easy believism or quick prayerism, but is actually to resurrect the ancient controversy of the Antinomians in all its tired failures and bankruptcy.

God's first attempt to restore mankind, that sin was merely an impurity or failure to attain to this restorative effort, and that God directed only pity on the sinner rather than wrath.[38] Not only a friend and pupil of the German Reformer, Martin Luther, Agricola was also a preacher and distinguished headmaster of a Latin school in Eisleben. His commentary soon caught the attention of another young protégé of Luther's, a Luther-appointed professor at the University of Wittenberg by the name of Philip Melanchthon, credited with being the first systematic theologian of the Protestant Reformation and the co-founder of Lutheranism.[39]

Melanchthon took it upon himself to respond to these troubling deviations in 1527 with his *Articles of Visitation* and later in the 1530 *Augsburg Confession*, countering that sin was forgiven upon contrition and faith, "for Christ's sake," that the law must be preached for the conviction of sinners, and that repentance precedes faith in bringing about the free gift of grace.[40] The intent of publishing this treatise was to check Agricola's aberrant ideas before they blossomed into something more. But they were not well received as such. Upon publication of this statement, Agricola immediately began showing signs of hostility towards Melanchthon, prompting intervention by Luther, himself. At a meeting in Torgau in November of 1527, Luther discussed the matter between the two theologians and asked the two men to clarify their beliefs.[41] Surely, there could be no disagreement among this close circle of reformers on something as fundamental as the gospel. Perhaps it was only a matter of rhetoric and semantics.

Little is known as to what was said in this meeting, but the hostility was apparently smoothed over, and Luther seemed satisfied that Agricola was not preaching a false gospel. All was well on the surface. But deep down, Agricola still maintained a fundamentally different view of the law and the gospel, and he continued disseminating his unbiblical teachings among other friends and colleagues. For years, rumors of this disagreement continued to emanate from Eisleben back to Luther, who generally ignored them as untrue and did his best to maintain friendly relations with Agricola.[42]

But three printed sermons were anonymously circulated within the University of Wittenberg in the mid-1530s that fiercely denounced the teachings of Melancthon and Luther on the issue of repentance, the law, and the gospel. Attacking the two reformers by name, Agricola anonymously accused Melancthon and Luther of teaching a false gospel by confusing the role of the law in converting the sinner. Agricola argued that the good news of the gospel alone was sufficient to convert the sinner, with no need of mentioning the law.[43] In 1537, he revealed himself by publicly preaching a sermon to this effect. It was at this point that Luther saw Agricola as the true foe he had become.[44] Most likely, it was at this point that Luther realized the issue was not just one of semantics, but rather the problem of a completely foreign and false gospel. An outright heretic had gone undetected in their midst for years.

Luther reluctantly withdrew his support from Agricola upon confirmation that his protégé had indeed been disseminating unorthodox and unbiblical views of the gospel. He withdrew his imprimatur from one of Agricola's books and stopped the printing of a series of gospel summaries Agricola had penned. Even still, Luther attempted to reconcile with him. But Agricola responded by boldly accusing the great reformer of teaching two gospels. On one hand, there was the Martin Luther who had pointed his finger at Rome and proclaimed, "The just shall live by faith." On the other hand was the Martin Luther who was now teaching that the law played a role in saving the just. In Agricola's characterization, Martin Luther was simultaneously preaching salvation by grace alone and also by works plus faith. He demanded that Luther declare which one was the true gospel.

Martin Luther's Pendulum

Martin Luther is often decried by some for his errors, of which there are undeniably several. His fierce opposition to the Baptists and his confusion about the Eucharist stand out as some of his worst flaws. It is not my intent to either deify this man or overlook his errors. Yet neither is it my intent to pretend that he did not bring about the greatest mass exodus from the Roman Catholic clutches in the past two thousand years or that he was not one of the greatest articulators of soteriology ever to print a page. That being said, it should be noted that Martin Luther is also very misunderstood at times, due to his balanced approach to many issues, an approach which is often mistaken by those in one of the two extremes who sometimes characterize him as siding with the other. In some cases, he is quoted completely out of context to paint him as advocating the complete opposite of what his teachings actually promoted. It was true that a young Martin Luther placed much of his emphasis on the doctrine of free grace, while an older Martin Luther spoke often about the need for the law. But consider the context he faced in each of these life phases. These were not two gospels, but rather responses to two different heresies prevailing at two different times in Luther's life. Allow his own words to defend him:

> True it is that at the early stage of this movement we began strenuously to teach the gospel and made use of these words which the Antinomians now quote. But the circumstances of that time were very different from those of the present day. Then the world was terrorized enough when the pope or the visage of a single priest shook the whole of Olympus, not to mention earth and hell, over all which that man of sin had usurped the power to himself. To the consciences of men so

oppressed, terrified, miserable, anxious, and afflicted, there was no need to inculcate the law. The clamant need then was to present the other part of the teaching of Christ in which he commands us to preach the remission of sin in his name, so that those who were already sufficiently terrified might learn not to despair, but to take refuge in the grace and mercy offered in Christ. Now, however, when the times are very dissimilar from those under the pope, our Antinomians – those suave theologians – retain our words, our doctrine, the joyful tidings concerning Christ, and wish to preach this alone, not observing that men are other than they were under that hangman, the pope, and have become secure, froward, wicked violators – yea, Epicureans who neither fear God nor men. Such men they confirm and comfort by their doctrine. In those days we were terrorized so that we trembled even at the fall of a leaf…But now our softly singing Antinomians, paying no attention to the change of the times, make men secure who are of themselves already so secure that they fall away from grace…Our view hitherto has been and ought to be this salutary one – if you see the afflicted and contrite, preach grace as much as you can. But not to the secure, the slothful, the harlots, adulterers, and blasphemers.[45]

These were not two gospels, but rather responses to two different heresies prevailing at two different times in Luther's life.

This is the approach clearly borne out by Scripture: law to the proud; grace to the humble. In James 4:6, the Bible says, "God resisteth the proud, but giveth grace unto the humble." When the rich young ruler came to Jesus thinking himself good enough to be saved, Christ gave him yet another commandment to observe: "If thou wilt be perfect, go and sell that thou hast, and give to the poor."[46] Where sinners are already penitent and looking for mercy, it is biblical to give them mercy and grace. But where sinners are haughty and proud in their perceived liberty (or self-righteousness), it is biblical to condemn them with God's law and wrath. Thus, when Rome thundered to the poor that they must work to be saved, Luther preached free grace. But when the pendulum had swung to the opposite extreme, and *Libertines* were teaching liberty

"But now our softly singing Antinomians, paying no attention to the change of the times, make men secure who are of themselves already so secure that they fall away from grace."

to sin, Luther preached God's law. This was the only consistent, biblical approach that Luther could choose. In his 1539 *Against the Antinomians*, Luther went on to explain this distinction, noting that removing wrath from the message would handicap sinners from knowing how to properly respond to conviction should it ever fall upon them:

> But the devil devotes himself to making men secure, teaching them to heed neither law nor sin, so that if sometime they were suddenly overtaken by death or by a bad conscience, they have grown so accustomed to nothing but sweet security that they sink helplessly into hell. For they have learned to perceive nothing in Christ but sweet security. Therefore such terror must be a sure sign that Christ (whom they understand as sheer sweetness) has rejected and forsaken them. That is what the devil strives for, and that is what he would like to see.
>
> It seems to me that these spirits think that all who are listening to the message are pure Christians, without sin – though in reality they are dejected and downcast hearts who feel their sin and fear God and who therefore must be comforted. To such, the dear Jesus can never be portrayed sweetly enough.[47]

Attempts to End the Controversy

In response to Agricola's accusations and criticism, Luther drafted two sets of written disputations and defended them in a public setting in 1537 and 1538. These theses outlined the various arguments of Agricola and his Antinomians and refuted them one at a time. At the end of the second public disputation, Agricola consented to Luther's arguments and confessed his error. Two more disputations were already being printed and were soon released, but not debated publicly, due to the reconciliation between the two factions.[48]

However, upon circulation of a new rumor that Agricola was merely biding his time until Luther died to then publicly preach the antinomian gospel, Luther printed a fifth set of theses that culminated in another flare-up and another public disputation in late 1538. This disputation seemed to put a nail in the coffin of Agricola's Antinomianism, and he began a written retraction. Philip Melanchthon, finding the retraction to be measured and incomplete, reworked it and suggested the edits to Agricola. Perhaps because the rivalry was too sharp between the two theologians, Agricola refused Melanchthon's reworked version and instead asked Luther, himself, to write a retraction for him. This he did in 1539 in the form of his now-famous *Against the Antinomians*, a scorching treatise on the wickedness and indefensible nature of this heresy. It was so strongly worded that Agricola took offense and retracted his retraction and circumnavigated Luther's authority to then become dean of the college of liberal arts at Wittenberg, leaving Eisleben.[49]

Agricola was once again rogue and on the attack. He brought suit against Luther for what he believed was slander in Luther's *Against the Antinomians* and another treatise the great reformer had penned, *Councils and Churches*.[50] The controversy had significantly escalated, as the founder of German Protestantism would be put on trial by his pupil, who had previously received the approval of the faculty at Wittenberg University when they appointed him dean over

Luther's opposition. The battle lines were drawn, and the conflict seemed ready to split the Lutheran movement.

Luther struck back with his own accusations against Agricola for his underhanded attempts to subvert Luther's authority at the university in addition to his secretive dissemination of heretical teachings contrary to those of the university, Luther, and the Bible.[51] Both in Eisleben and now at Wittenberg, Agricola had been underhanded in dealing with this situation, releasing anonymous assaults, both verbally and in print, against orthodoxy – all while pretending friendship and agreement with Luther, Melanchthon, and the faculty at Wittenberg. Luther charged him with being a kind of Judas, undermining the authority of the law and gospel while kissing them both when it best suited him. His several measured retractions of this heresy were now viewed by Luther and his supporters as insincere and mere tactics in overthrowing the teaching of the university in a bid to rewrite Lutheranism upon Luther's death.

As the trial neared, Count Albrecht of Mansfield wrote the university expressing his severe concern over Agricola, fearing he might seek to spread his poisonous doctrine in other areas besides Wittenberg and Eisleben. Although the faculty at Wittenberg had made him dean over Luther's opposition, they were not decidedly in Agricola's camp and chose to heed the count's wise warning. The elector at Wittenberg initiated a hearing with Agricola, which produced a solemn pledge from Agricola that he would not leave Wittenberg until the trial had run its course and either he or Luther had been vindicated.[52] Yet in 1540, in spite of the pledge he had given, Agricola accepted a position as court preacher in Berlin at the invitation of the elector at Brandenburg. Luther commented, upon receiving news that Agricola had fled rather than face complete and official repudiation, "Thus the tree is known by its fruits," calling him a "perfidious and abandoned man."[53]

But this was not the last Wittenberg would hear of Johannes Agricola. A few months later, he reached out to his old nemesis, Philip Melanchthon, to mediate between himself and Martin Luther.

In a stunning reversal, Agricola wrote out a complete recantation of Antinomianism, aptly entitled, *Confession and Affirmation of God's Law*.[54] Melanchthon obliged, but sent the recantation back, again concerned it was not worded strongly enough. This had happened once before, with an explosive outcome. But Agricola surprisingly implemented these changes and followed the program Melanchthon had suggested for the entire recantation. The strongly worded recantation confessed this heretical sin of Antinomianism in no uncertain terms and even explained how it had been arrived at.

Agricola wrote out a complete recantation of Antinomianism, aptly entitled, Confession and Affirmation of God's Law.

Agricola confessed that he had overreacted and become imbalanced in his doctrine from debating legalism with the Roman Catholics and their works-based gospel.[55] While Luther had emphasized free grace to the Catholics and then made the switch to emphasizing law and repentance to the Libertines, Agricola had become stuck in the anti-legalism rut and had not matured to the point of preaching a balanced perspective. He had never fully grasped grace to the humble and law to the proud. He apologized for this immature imbalance and the heretical ideas that grew from it.

Agricola boldly owned that it was Martin Luther's arguments that had convinced him of his error and taught him the proper balance between grace and law. Yes, salvation is freely given by grace through faith, yet it can only come after the sinner has laid down his weapons of war and repented of his sin upon encountering the preaching of God's law. His recantation was so full and complete this time, that it not only mended his relationship with those at Wittenberg, but completely offended his former, antinomian colleagues at Eisleben.[56] Though Luther maintained his skepticism of him, Agricola – the instigator of the First Antinomian Controversy – for all intents and purposes was a changed man and no longer an Antinomian.

Antinomian Teachings Then and Now

Today we have men rebuking those who preach the law of God and who tell sinners to repent of their sin and yield to Christ. These men preach a Hollywood message that all you have to do to be saved is "believe." And if met with any opposition from fellow Christians that this is not enough, the response is to "truly" believe. Well, what is true belief? After all, the Bible tells us in James 2 that even the devils "believe." Why is it now considered such an error to teach, as our forefathers taught, that true belief includes repentance from sin? What has happened in the past few generations that brought about such a radical notion that was virtually unheard of prior to the 1970s? Was this invented by Jack Hyles and First Baptist Church of Hammond, Indiana?

On the contrary, it is the premise of this work that the modern attack on the role of repentance in the gospel is nothing more than the contemporary embodiment of the ancient antinomian controversy, the descendant or heir of that once-refuted heresy. And to illustrate this, we shall examine the most common arguments of modern Antinomians and trace them back to their roots in the 16th century. We shall pull back the soil from the toxic tree of this modern enemy of the gospel and find that its roots go down directly to Agricola and the ancient Antinomians who were soundly and scripturally refuted so long ago.

Removing the Emphasis on Sin

One of the first things that becomes apparent when discussing the issue of repentance from sin with a modern Antinomian is their emphasis on salvation from hell rather than payment for sin. I once presented the biblical role of repentance in the gospel to a Bible study group I had been participating in for some time. The leader of the

Bible study had taken a hard stance against repentance, and for three hours I defended my position with the group, often clashing with this particular young man. At the end of three hours of trying to help these people see this biblical truth, the entire conversation became snagged on one very odd question: hell or sin? The entire debate had culminated in the question: which was the primary problem solved by the cross – man's sin or his danger of going to hell? I argued from Scripture that the cross was intended to pay the just penalty incurred by our sin, whereas this young man argued it was to save our hides from being burned in hell. As the debate heated up and Bible reference after Bible reference was rejected by this disturbingly humanistic young man, the three-hour discourse ended with him shouting out with all his might, "HELL!" To which I yelled back, "SIN!" And that was the end. This was the impasse that prevented any further debate. This was the crux of the entire disagreement summarized in just two words: hell and sin.

Modern Antinomians, just like their ancient counterparts, view the gospel through humanistic lenses. They see the entire issue of the gospel as a matter of saving souls from hell, whereas the Bible teaches that the whole point of the gospel was to pay the penalty for our sin and reconcile us to a holy God. Their disregard for God's perspective and holy law leads them to believe the whole point of Calvary was merely to rescue them from eternal suffering. And this is why repentance from sin is so repugnant to them. As the Lutheran apologist, Philip Melanchthon, observed in his *Articles of Visitation,* "Many now talk only about forgiveness of sins and say little or nothing about repentance."[57] And it is this point that identifies Antinomianism – lawlessness – as the true problem confronting the true gospel today. Having reduced their esteem of God's law, Antinomians no longer care that much about sin, because it has already been paid for and we are going to heaven.

A popular online preacher featured on the show, *Wretched,* with Todd Friel, in a video that has since been removed from the internet, once blasted repentance in the gospel and in so doing mocked those who try to make sin exceeding sinful. This Antinomian preacher admitted that sinners need to admit they are sinners when praying the sinner's prayer, but had the humanistic audacity to say they should not be encouraged to think of themselves as horrible, wicked sinners – just average, run-of-the-mill sinners. In his mind, sin was a very minor part of the story of redemption. A recent online discussion with a modern Antinomian regarding the need for sinners to repent of their sin in order to be ready for grace produced this comment, "You are way too worried about sin friend. It is paid for."

The modern attack on the role of repentance in the gospel is nothing more than the contemporary embodiment of the ancient antinomian controversy, the descendant or heir of that once-refuted heresy.

And where would these enemies of repentance get such a casual attitude towards sin? Where might they have picked up such a flippant view of that which crucified the Son of God? From their ancient Antinomian counterparts, of course. As recorded in the *Lutheran Cyclopedia*, Agricola – the founder of the ancient Antinomian cult – had a curiously unbiblical view of sin, regarding it "as a malady or impurity rather than an offense rendering the sinner guilty and damnable before God."[58] Surely, if your philosophy descends from the school of thought that sin is not really the transgression of God's holy law, but merely a weakness or imperfection, you may easily find it offensive to think that God would require you to denounce it in order to be offered the free gift of grace. Surely, if sin is just an impurity that you will eventually grow out of, you can continue in that sin and get saved. No need to put that dagger of rebellion down.

In his preeminent work on this subject, *Repentance and Soul-Winning*, evangelist and author, David Cloud, wrote about his experience as a missionary in South Asia and a conversation he had with a man who wanted to be saved. The businessman was concerned, however, about how to go about this while retaining a mistress and shady business practices.   Many Antinomians would see no problem with this – after all, sin is just an imperfection that can be dealt with after salvation. But David Cloud rightly "told him that he was going to have to repent of his sin and BE WILLING for God to take control."[59] In the same book, Cloud recounts a conversation that took place between a pastor friend of his and an Antinomian pastor.   The Antinomian

> *"If you are completely and deeply engrossed in sin, if you believe, you are in the midst of salvation."*

pastor was asked what he would do if dealing with a reprobate like the basketball star, Dennis Rodman, who hypothetically wanted to be saved but specifically refused to give up any sins – would this pastor lead him in the sinner's prayer? The Antinomian pastor responded, "Yes."[60]

Again, we must ask, from where does such an impudent gospel arise – a treasonous gospel that allows a mere profession of faith to admit a sinner, still openly engaged in sinful warfare against God, into the kingdom of heaven? And again, to find the root of this modern heresy, we have only to read the words of the ancient Antinomian, Agricola, who audaciously concluded that, "If you are completely and deeply engrossed in sin, if you believe, you are in the midst of salvation."[61]

Removing Wrath from the Gospel

If those who reject the role of repentance in the gospel do not see sin as the primary problem solved by the gospel, then it only follows that many of them will also de-emphasize God's righteous wrath and indignation toward that sin. The Bible teaches us that it is both the goodness and severity of God that should be preached to sinners to motivate them to be converted. The Bible speaks of this dual incentive to obey the gospel:

And of some have compassion, making a difference: And
others save with fear, pulling them out of the fire; hating
even the garment spotted by the flesh.

Jude 22-23

But many of those who reject repentance in the gospel prefer
we do not talk about the judgment and wrath of God, lest we turn
sinners off to the goodness and mercy of God. In other words, they
insist we only use compassion and a positive message to win souls,
leaving the "turn or burn" message out of it. Their aversion to talking
about negative things like hell is ironic, considering they typically
emphasize saving souls from hell as the primary purpose of the
gospel rather than reconciling the sinner to God or paying their sin
debt. But this aversion to mentioning hell in the gospel presentation
is nevertheless common among them. They often shy away from
emphasizing hell, damnation, God's law, or anything negative when
talking to the sinner. Everything must be positive, upbeat, and bunny
rabbits.

Take, for example, this utterly unbiblical and grotesquely
"positive" method taught by the man Jack Hyles called the world's
greatest soul-winner, Carl Hatch:

> I don't ask anybody if they want to be saved. If you want
> a positive answer you must ask a positive question. If you
> want a no answer ask a no question. If you want a yes
> answer ask a yes question. Soul winning is positive. And
> in soul winning you use a lot of reverse psychology and
> psychology.
> For instance, if you are lost and I say, "Mr. Smith, let me ask
> you a question. You don't want to go to hell, do you?" He
> will answer, No.
> I say, "Wonderful, you want to go to heaven, don't you?"
> He will say yes. I will reply, "Sure you do. Sure you do.
> Sure you do. Sure you do. I thank God for a man that
> doesn't want to go to hell."
> Did you get that? I am reinforcing the fact that he wants to

go to heaven. I'm keep (sic) everything positive.

I don't say, "Can I show this to you?" or "Do you mind if I read the Bible to you?" That's negative and you will probably get a negative answer. I don't ask people; I just say, "I'm so glad you don't want to go to hell and I will just take a minute here to show you some verses. I don't have long and I know you don't, either. There's three things that you need to know. First, Jesus died for you. Isn't that wonderful? Two, Jesus loves you. Isn't that wonderful? Three, Jesus wants you to go to heaven. Isn't that wonderful? And I'm so glad that you want to."

See, I am being positive.

He may say he has a lot of questions, but unsaved people don't have questions. Don't get on unsaved people's questions. Tell them that you will answer their questions later, but first you want to read a few verses of Scripture. Unsaved people don't have questions. If you get them saved, that answers all of them.

"And if he doesn't repeat that and tries not to pray, I squeeze his shoulder."

Let me tell you how to deal with someone who has a dumb spirit who bucks getting saved. You share the gospel and get them to the point of praying the sinner's prayer, but they stop. How do you get that type of person saved? Now, this will work in most cases. If he is a man, put your hand on his shoulder and say, "Mr. Jones, I want to have prayer for you. I'm thrilled you want to go to heaven. God has been good to you. Bow your head with me. Then I pray, "Lord, I'm so thankful for this man that doesn't want to burn in hell. I'm so thrilled he wants to go to heaven and not take his kids to hell. I thank you for this man. And I pray you will help him to see that need." While our heads are still bowed, I say, "Mr. Jones, if you want heaven as your home and Christ as your Saviour, pray this prayer. Lord Jesus." And if he doesn't repeat that and tries not to pray, I squeeze his shoulder. I use this technique. If I am dealing with the president of the bank, I take his hand and when it comes time for him to pray, I squeeze his hand. We've titled that the Carl Hatch squeeze. It works. If I am dealing with a woman, I ask her to put her hand on the Bible, and when it comes time to pray I just tap her hand gently. It works; it works.[62]

Such unbiblical and manipulative methodology is enough to make a con artist blush. Another modern Antinomian pastor and author by the name of Dr. Paul Ellis writes of repentance, "Repentance is one of the most important things you'll ever do but it's not worth an entire sermon."[63] Echoing this common theme that repentance and the law of God are simply technicalities that should not be emphasized because they are too negative, Dr. Ellis goes on with this nugget:

> To get people to repent (change their minds) Jesus preached the good news of the kingdom. He painted a picture of where God wanted them to be (with Him here and now) and He gave them clear directions on how to get there (have faith in God). It was the same with Paul. He didn't walk into Corinth, one of the world's most depraved cities, and preach "turn from sin." Instead he resolved to know nothing but "Christ and Him crucified" (1 Cor 2:2). Sinners need to learn how much God loves them. They need to hear about His unconditional favor and grace.

Is this a new teaching? It is certainly not to be found in the Bible, but is it only a recent deviation from the Scriptures or an ancient strand that trails all the way back to Mother Antinomianism? It is not difficult to see the answer is the latter. Two of the earliest points made by Agricola and his Antinomian followers of long ago are:

> Therefore, in order to preserve the purity of doctrine one must resist those who teach that the Gospel is not to be preached except to souls that first have been crushed and made contrite by the law.
> For they add to the words of Christ this improper sermon and teach that first the law needs to be taught, then the

Gospel. These are the distorters of Christ's words, for they do not abide by the simplicity of the words of Christ.[64]

In their ancient heresy, the Antinomians made much of the fact that faith was mentioned before wrath in the first chapter of Romans, ignoring the pattern of the overall book and showing themselves to be the spiritual forefathers of the Dr. Paul Ellises and Carl Hatches of today. Martin Luther had this to say of this frivolous hermeneutic:

> They have devised for themselves a new method whereby one is to preach grace first and then the revelation of wrath. The word "law" is not to be heard or spoken. This is a nice little toy from which they derive much pleasure. They claim they can fit the entire Scripture into this pattern and thus they become the light of the world. That is the meaning they foist on St. Paul in Romans 1:18. But they fail to see that he teaches just the opposite. First he calls attention to the wrath of God from heaven and makes all the world sinners and guilty before God; then, after they have become sinners, he teaches them how to obtain mercy and be justified. That is what the first three chapters powerfully and clearly demonstrate.[65]

Popular internet preacher and pastor, Steven Anderson, who attended Hyles-Anderson College, is currently one of the most vitriolic and well-known opponents of repentance in the gospel online. He founded and maintains a website directory of preachers who preach that sinners must repent of their sin to be saved, called the *Repentance Blacklist* (a list on which this author's name appears).[66] In his sermon, *Repent of Your Sins Heresy*,[67] Anderson echoes a very specific strain of ancient Antinomianism by rejecting the role of conviction in bringing a sinner to the point of salvation. He points out, "The word 'convicted' is only used one time in the entire Bible, and guess what, the people who were convicted went to hell." Anderson proceeds to read the passage in John regarding the woman caught in adultery and concludes that the Pharisees who accused the woman and were "convicted" according to scripture died and went to hell. He then extrapolates that conviction is not something sinners need if they are to be saved, but rather is something God brings upon those who are damned and without hope of salvation. He therefore concludes that sinners do not need to be brought to the point of feeling guilty, as long as they can clinically agree in a technical sense that they are, indeed, guilty. He adds:

> Conviction is a guilty feeling in your own heart. Do you
> have to have a guilty feeling [to be saved]? No. You have
> to acknowledge your guilt, but you don't have to have a
> guilty feeling.[68]

He then directs his audience's attention to John 16:8, where Christ says the Comforter (Holy Ghost) will "reprove the world of sin," and proceeds in a mocking tone of voice to caricature repentance preachers and question whether this passage is really talking about conviction of sin (which the text plainly says) or of unbelief:

> Now, let's see if this is really being convicted of your sins,
> you know, here, you know, where you feel bad, because
> you've been, you know, living a sinful life, and, you, you've
> broken God's commandments, and you've been drinking,
> and you've been, you've been a drunk, and you've been a,
> uh, a deadbeat, and you've been an adulterer, and you've
> been a fornicator, and you've been covetous, and your life
> is ruled by the love of money, and you've been stealing, and
> you've been skipping church, and you don't read the Bible,
> and you blaspheme God's name, and now you finally feel
> bad about it. Nope...So what is the reproving the world of
> sin about? Because they believed not on Him.[69]

The passage says, "Of sin, because they believe not on me," clearly showing that sin is the problem and that believing on Christ will prevent the sinner from having to pay for that sin. But Anderson the Antinomian teaches that it actually means the exact opposite – that no one has to pay for their sins, that unbelief is the only thing that merits God's reproof, and that sinners should not have to feel guilty for all these wicked sins against God in order to be a candidate for grace. Never mind the fact that the Bible declares in Ephesians that it truly is sin that brings about the judgment of God (hell):

> For this ye know, that no whoremonger, nor unclean person, nor covetous man, who is an idolater, hath any inheritance in the kingdom of Christ and of God. Let no man deceive you with vain words: for because of these things cometh the wrath of God upon the children of disobedience.[70]

Never mind entire passages of Scripture, like this passage from Romans, that explain to us the working of God's law in smiting the sinner's heart with guilt and magnifying the sinfulness of his sin:

> What shall we say then? Is the law sin? God forbid. Nay, I had not known sin, but by the law: for I had not known lust, except the law had said, Thou shalt not covet.
> But sin, taking occasion by the commandment, wrought in me all manner of concupiscence. For without the law sin was dead.
> For I was alive without the law once: but when the commandment came, sin revived, and I died.
> And the commandment, which was ordained to life, I found to be unto death.
> For sin, taking occasion by the commandment, deceived me, and by it slew me.
> Wherefore the law is holy, and the commandment holy, and just, and good.
> Was then that which is good made death unto me? God forbid. But sin, that it might appear sin, working death in me by that which is good; that sin by the commandment might become exceeding sinful.[71]

Where does Anderson get such unbiblical ideas about conviction? Is this some new idea that the sinner should not be led to feel guilty of his sin in encountering the gospel? Did he invent the notion that the law only convicts to damnation? Or can this, too, be traced back to the ancient Antinomians of Eisleben?

"Let no man deceive you with vain words: for because of these things cometh the wrath of God upon the children of disobedience."

The answer to these questions can be easily found in the very first disputation of the ancient Antinomian Controversy. The 16th point of Agricola's initial antinomian teachings stated in plain terms, "The law only convicts of sin and is certainly without the Holy Spirit; therefore it convicts to damnation."[72] In a book by Timothy J. Wengert, as reviewed by Lowell C. Green, Agricola went so far in his preaching on Colossians as to put it this way:

> Philosophy says, "When you sin, you are condemned; be afraid!" God's word says, "When you sin, be happy. It is to have no consequence. Sin does not condemn you; good works do not save you, but rather faith in Jesus Christ alone." For this reason, then, there is in the congregation forgiveness of sins without ceasing.[73]

The apple does not fall far from the tree.

Removing Repentance

The Antinomians of today and yesterday seem to wish to do away with repentance altogether. When dealing with modern opponents of repentance in the gospel, one will often hear something along the lines of, "Could you give the gospel without using the word, *repent*?" or "Many salvation verses in the Bible do not even mention repentance." They will even stoop to such illogical argumentation as to point out that the exact phrase, "repent of your sins," does not appear in Scripture, in spite of the fact that repentance from sin is taught throughout Scripture, just using slightly different phraseology. Likewise, they make much ado about the fact that the word, *repent*, does not appear in the entire book of John and thus must not be important. Dr. Don Boyd, an evangelist out of Jack Hyles' church in Hammond, Indiana, used such arguments. In his sermon, *What Persuasion Are You?*, he asked his audience:

> How many of you have heard somebody preach on this subject, "repent of your sins?"...That is not mentioned in the Bible one time. Show me in the Gospel of John the word, "repent." It's not in there.[74]

Never mind that also not appearing in the book of John are terms like "virgin birth," "trinity," "redemption," and "hell." So the question bears asking, should we likewise throw out all these doctrines, simply because these exact words do not appear in the book of John?

This is not proper hermeneutics, and it betrays a not-so-subtle disdain for the doctrine of repentance as found in the Bible. But it is not new. Indeed, Martin Luther, in the very *First Disputation* of the ancient Antinomian Controversy, addressed the question put forth by the original Antinomians, "Show me, please, where Christ commanded to preach the law." They were arguing that, while some verses taught that we should preach repentance, the preaching of the law was not to be associated with the preaching of repentance, because the law and repentance are totally separate terms. To them, preaching repentance was simply preaching the gospel of faith without discussing sin, since Christ never used the exact term they required. Luther responded:

> It is true according to grammar and when the words are taken materially or strictly. For grammatically, repentance and law are two different words, but as to the subject matter, it is the same to preach repentance and to preach the law... For even if we do not put down these letters, L-A-W, we are still looking at the thing itself...We are not concerned about the word, "law," but about the thing itself.[75]

Luther also faced the all-too-common accusation that he was teaching a works-based gospel. Yes, the man universally remembered for insisting that "the just shall live by faith" was accused of preaching works salvation for the same reason modern Antinomians accuse those who, like Luther, insist that the law of God is perfect, converting the soul. Literally every person, today, who opposes repentance in the gospel echoes this ancient accusation in attempting to throw out this crucial doctrine. Jack Hyles, in his book, *Enemies of Soul-Winning*, was no exception to this rule. Consider these statements of his:

> If we must make Jesus Lord of our lives in order to be saved, then salvation is not all of grace.[76]

> If one has to be changed to be saved, that's salvation by works.[77]

Likewise, in late 1537, the man who had defied Rome in all her pomp and circumstance for the sake of salvation by grace through faith alone received a letter from his protégé, Johannes Agricola, accusing him of "teaching two manners of justification: one through the law and faith; the other through the gospel alone."[78] Some things never change.

Redefining Repentance

When the doctrine of repentance cannot be successfully thrown out, de-emphasized, or robbed of its companion elements, such as wrath and the law, it is often redefined by the Hyles crowd and those who subscribe to his philosophy. Rather than stick with the biblical definition of repentance as a change of heart and mind regarding actions, committed or intended, that results in a change of course, it is now taken as meaning nothing more than believing in Christ. In other words, whereas the Bible teaches that sinners must turn from their sin and turn to the Savior, now some insist that sinners must only turn from unbelief to belief, making for a rather redundant gospel in such places as Mark 1:15, which in their minds reads, "The time is fulfilled, and the kingdom of God is at hand: believe ye, and believe the gospel." Today, numerous preachers and fundamentalist Christians echo this perversion of repentance resurrected in the late 20th century by none other than Jack Hyles, who stated:

> There are those who say we have to repent of our sins in order to be saved. No, we have to repent only of the thing that makes us unsaved, and that is unbelief.[79]

> When we put our faith and trust in Christ, and repent of unbelief, and believe, God's Holy Spirit comes in to live and begins to straighten us out.[80]

> Repenting from the thing that makes you lost is the thing that makes you saved, and that is, repenting of your unbelief.[81]

> Jesus Himself is saying repent, and notice immediately He says, "repent, and believe." What He was saying is, "Quit unbelieving, and believe. Quit not believing and believe."[82]

Though that may be sufficient rhetorical gymnastics to make anyone dizzy, it is surprisingly not original. Jack Hyles was only parroting the foolishness he learned from his ancient antinomian forbears. In the mind of Hyles and all Antinomians, old and new, the problem is not sin, it is unbelief. See if these antinomian statements included in the *First Disputation* sound familiar:

> In the Gospel we are not to deal with doing violence to the law, but with doing violence to the Son.[83]

> Peter taught repentance from the profaning of the Son. Peter was a preacher. Therefore, preachers should teach repentance from the profaning of the Son, not from the Law of Moses.[84]

And so, to Agricola and his followers, the gospel presentation should not discuss transgressing the law (sin), but should only discuss what the sinner will do with Jesus (belief vs. unbelief). The question of sin damning us to hell now becomes irrelevant. The command to the sinner ceases to be a command to put down the sinful dagger of rebellion and flee into the arms of a merciful God and becomes a meaningless question of whether or not the sinner believes in Jesus (in a nondescript way), much in the same meaningless way the devils of James 2 believe in Him. And to this point, Martin Luther had a very interesting and profound rebuttal. In essence, Luther argued that, if one does not need to repent of sin to be saved and sin does not damn us to hell, then sin is better than righteousness and belief in Christ is unnecessary. This complex argument is profound and must not be overlooked. For Luther here shows how Antinomianism overturns the gospel completely. Follow his syllogism carefully:

Jack Hyles was only parroting the foolishness he learned from his ancient antinomian forbears.

> Here it becomes apparent that they want to teach such a sin that does not condemn, that perhaps even saves without Christ.
> For if sin does not damn, it remains that Christ has not redeemed us from damning sin, therefore also not from God's wrath.
> Sin that does not damn is a sin better than righteousness itself and life.
> For what is more blessed than having a sin that does not damn, that is, a sin that does not exist.
> Therefore, with the law removed, we are thus saved from sin, so that we do not even need Christ as mediator etc.[85]

His argument extends somewhat beyond the scope of our topic at hand, and yet it is very pertinent to our discussion and worthy of close examination. He is essentially arguing that, with the law removed from the equation, and with sin no longer being what damns the sinner, and with the whole point of repentance now only being a matter of believing or not believing, what then is the problem with sin? Why is it a problem at all? In fact, what could be better than a sin that does not damn and therefore require our belief in Christ? Here Luther is arguing that, if we remove the law from the gospel, and turning from sin from the definition of repentance, we have removed the very thing that necessitates our belief in Christ! If repentance only means embracing Jesus with the knife of sin still clutched in our hands, and Jesus is ok with our sin and just wants us to embrace Him, why then do we need to embrace Him at all? On what grounds could He damn us, since sin is not damnable?

This is a powerful critique of the antinomian position and thoroughly decimates the very core of its philosophy. Sin is what damns us to hell and requires faith in a Savior. And unless we relinquish our sin and run to the Savior in absolute trust, our sin retains its power to damn us eternally. But when Antinomianism removes sin from the equation, the gospel implodes. The antinomian gospel is thus self-refuting. And so we see that the Antinomianism of today is much the same as the Antinomianism of yesterday: completely destitute of reason and truth.

Chapter 3

A FIRM FOUNDATION

Thou shalt not remove thy neighbour's landmark,
which they of old time have set in thine inheritance,
which thou shalt inherit in the land that the Lord thy
God giveth thee to possess it.

Deuteronomy 19:14

Before delving deeply into the myriad of scriptures on this topic to determine what the words of God dictate, let us first establish that this inclusion of repentance in the gospel has always been the orthodox foundation upon which the Church has stood for two thousand years. With a few notable exceptions throughout history, God's preachers have typically thundered an anti-sin message of repentance from their pulpits and books. Sin was the disease, but Christ had the cure. It is this tradition and orthodoxy that should be preserved. Certainly, the words of men do not prove anything, and our hope is not in man. Yet when viewing the landscape of Christendom over the centuries, we see a clear and marked pattern of consistency – a guide, if you will, that we can line up with God's Word to determine the boundaries and confines of our soteriology thus setting our feet on solid rock.

The Principle of Orthodoxy

When writing about the New Testament Church he was so instrumental in founding, the great apostle, Peter, compared the saints to Christ as integral parts of its foundation. While Christ is certainly the chief cornerstone and Rock of our salvation, He has chosen us, as well, as precious stones making up the structure of the Church. Calling the Church a "house," Peter includes the saints in its construction:

> Ye also, as lively stones, are built up a spiritual house, an holy priesthood, to offer up spiritual sacrifices, acceptable to God by Jesus Christ.[86]

In determining the importance and significance of faith (defined as "evidence,"[87] in and of itself), the author of Hebrews calls on the examples of many Old Testament saints and then rests his case on their witness, urging the reader to accept their witness as sufficient and move on:

> Wherefore seeing we also are compassed about with so great a cloud of witnesses, let us lay aside every weight, and the sin which doth so easily beset us, and let us run with patience the race that is set before us.[88]

He does not choose this term, "witnesses," lightly. Most likely, the writer here is the apostle Paul,[89] a Pharisee of the Pharisees well versed in the Holy Scriptures, laying out his case like an attorney. He uses this term in reference to a principle well established in old times – the principle of establishing a matter by witnesses. This rule, echoed by Jesus in Matthew 18:16, was first set forth in Deuteronomy:

> One witness shall not rise up against a man for any iniquity, or for any sin, in any sin that he sinneth: at the mouth of two witnesses, or at the mouth of three witnesses, shall the matter be established.
>
> Deuteronomy 19:15

This principle of determining truth by the word of two or three witnesses carried over into the New Testament as the principle of *orthodoxy*. By it, we agree that all essential doctrine has been once revealed by the Savior to His saints from the beginning of His Church, and has been faithfully carried down from preacher to preacher, teacher to teacher, saint to saint, from the time of Christ until the present. This is why the Bible places such an emphasis on passing on doctrinal teaching from generation to generation – not because tradition trumps the Bible, as the heretical Roman Catholics believe, but because its concurrence with the Scriptures and the general (and not private) interpretation of these witnesses stand as vital confirmation that guides us in our search for truth. Observe what Paul tells to his own spiritual protégé, Timothy:

> And the things that thou hast heard of me among many witnesses, the same commit thou to faithful men, who shall be able to teach others also.[90]

There we have it so plainly iterated, the principle of orthodoxy in a nutshell. The mechanism behind this concept is simply that all truly born-again believers have the ultimate witness, the Holy Ghost, living within them and guiding them to discern between false interpretations and correct interpretations of Scripture. And

This principle of determining truth by the word of two or three witnesses carried over into the New Testament as the principle of orthodoxy.

therefore, if we see a particular interpretation of biblical repentance prominent in Christendom from generation to generation, this is indicative of the leading of the Holy Ghost in the Church and thus the mind of God on the matter. Consider the following passages:

> Howbeit when he, the Spirit of truth, is come, he will guide you into all truth: for he shall not speak of himself; but whatsoever he shall hear, that shall he speak: and he will shew you things to come.
>
> John 16:3

> He that believeth on the Son of God hath the witness in
> himself:
>
> I John 5:10

This principle of a witness verifying the words of God is so foundational that we find it throughout Scripture, even applying to God, Himself:

> This is he that came by water and blood, even Jesus Christ;
> not by water only, but by water and blood. And it is the
> Spirit that beareth witness, because the Spirit is truth.
> For there are three that bear record in heaven, the Father, the
> Word, and the Holy Ghost: and these three are one.
> And there are three that bear witness in earth, the Spirit, and
> the water, and the blood: and these three agree in one.
>
> I John 5:6-8

> And the Father himself, which hath sent me, hath borne
> witness of me. Ye have neither heard his voice at any time,
> nor seen his shape.
>
> John 5:37

> Nevertheless he left not himself without witness, in that
> he did good, and gave us rain from heaven, and fruitful
> seasons, filling our hearts with food and gladness.
>
> Acts 14:17

And so we must conclude from this emphasis on witnesses and verification, that interpretations of Scripture are confirmed by the witness of the faithful men who have for generations heard the voice of the Spirit of truth and passed their knowledge on to future generations of believers in an everlasting house of God, comprised of saints through the ages. That in the mouth of their witness, every doctrine may be established, not as a primary evidence, but certainly as a secondary evidence. And in subsequent chapters of this work, the doctrine of repentance from sin will be proven beyond a shadow of a doubt from Scripture, the most important authority of all. But first, a brief survey of what these witnesses of God have taught over the years is without a doubt in order.

So Great a Cloud of Witnesses

Soon after the time of John the Beloved, in the 2nd and 3rd centuries AD, church father, Tertullian, was one of the most prolific writers on the theology of the new Christian faith. In his work, *On Repentance*, Tertullian emphasized that repentance from sins, far from being a work, would in fact bring about a merciful pardon:

> To all sins, then, committed whether by flesh or spirit, whether by deed or will, the same God who has destined penalty by means of judgment, has withal engaged to grant pardon by means of repentance, saying to the people, "Repent thee, and I will save thee;" and again, "I live, saith the Lord, and I will (have) repentance rather than death."[91]

Tertullian later contradicts the modern heresy that repentance is merely from unbelief, describing it emphatically as "repentance of (past) sins." After defining it so, he goes on to insist that this repentance is commanded by God:

> "Is it good to repent, or no?" Why do you ponder? God enjoins; nay, He not merely enjoins, but likewise exhorts. He invites by (offering) reward – salvation, to wit; even by an oath, saying "I live," He desires that credence may be given Him. Oh blessed we, for whose sake God swears! Oh most miserable, if we believe not the Lord even when He swears! What, therefore, God so highly commends, what He even (after human fashion) attests on oath, we are bound of course to approach, and to guard with the utmost seriousness.[92]

Before the Protestant Reformation, there existed many groups of true believers who dissented from Rome entirely and preserved the pure teachings of Christ. Among them were the *Waldensians*, a sect commonly accepted as Baptistic in doctrine. While they eventually apostatized, for many generations, they were a uniquely pure and authentic representative of Christ's bride on this earth. Their statement of faith of 1544 shows their position on repentance and conversion plainly. Pay special attention to the last three words:

> We believe that in the ordinance of baptism the water is the visible and external sign, which represents to us that which, by virtue of God's invisible operation, is within us – namely, the renovation of our minds, and the mortification of our members through [the faith of] Jesus Christ. And by this ordinance we are received into the holy congregation of God's people, previously professing and declaring our faith and change of life.[93]

The great martyr and Bible translator, William Tyndale, to whom we are indebted for much of the wording of our *King James* translation of the Holy Bible, wrote extensively on repentance in his "To the Reader" of 1534. Notice his definition encompasses four primary elements, including confession, contrition, faith, and satisfaction (works meet for repentance):

> Concerning this word repentance...the very sense and signification both of the Hebrew and also of the Greek word is, "to be converted and to turn to God with all the heart, to know his will, and to live according to his laws; and to be cured of our corrupt nature with the oil of his Spirit, and wine of obedience to his doctrine." Which conversion or turning, if it be unfeigned, these four do accompany it and are included therein: Confession, not in the priest's ear, for that is but man's invention, but to God in the heart, and before all the congregation of God; how that we be sinners and sinful, and that our whole nature is corrupt, and inclined to sin and all unrighteousness, and therefore evil, wicked, and damnable; and his Law holy and just, by which our sinful nature is rebuked: and also to our neighbours (sic), if we have offended any person particularly. Then Contrition,

sorrowfulness that we be such damnable sinners, and not only have sinned but are wholly inclined to sin still. Thirdly, Faith (of which our old doctors have made no mention at all in the description of their penance), that God for Christ's sake doth forgive us, and receive us to mercy, and is at one with us, and will heal our corrupt nature. And fourthly, Satisfaction, or amends-making, not to God with holy works, but to my neighbor whom I have hurt, and to the congregation of God, whom I have offended, (if any open crime be found in me); and submitting of a man's self unto the congregation or church of Christ, and to the officers of the same, to have his life corrected and governed henceforth of them.[94]

In the late 1600s, America's first true Baptist and the pastor of possibly the first Baptist church in the nation,[95] Roger Williams, decried the practice of giving the gospel to unrepentant people and not requiring an outward change as an evidence of an inner change:

Gospel Church must be made up of such regenerate men, and calls them actual believers, true disciples and converts, living stones, such as can give some account how the grace of God hath appeared unto them and wrought that heavenly change in them.[96]

He later wrote about his evangelism with the America Indians and answered the question of why he did not lead them in a cheap and easy conversion:

Woe be to me, if I call light darkness, or darkness light; sweet bitter, or bitter sweet; woe to me, if I call that conversion unto God, which is, indeed, subversion of the souls of millions in Christendom, from one worship to another, and the profanation of the holy name of God, his holy Son and blessed ordinances...I mean such a convert as is acceptable to God in Jesus Christ according to the visible rule of his last will and testament. I speak not of hypocrites, which may but glitter, and be no solid gold, as Simon Magus,

Judas, etc. But of a true external conversion I say, then, woe be to me! if intending to catch men, as the Lord Jesus said to Peter, I should pretend conversion, and the bringing of men, as mystical fish, into a Church estate, that is, a converted estate, and so build them up with ordinances as a converted Christian people...First, it must be by the free proclaiming and preaching of repentance and forgiveness of sins...as in the turning of the whole man from the power of Satan unto God. Acts 16. Such a change, as if an old man became a new babe (John 4); yea, as amounts to God's new creation in the soul.[97]

One of the greatest Baptist preachers of all time was Charles H. Spurgeon, known as the prince of preachers. He was an avid scholar and evangelistic pastor in the 1800s. His preaching on repentance is legendary:

First, we cannot be saved without repentance. No remission of sin can be given without repentance. The two things are so joined together by God, as they are in our text, that they cannot be separated. Many mistakes are made as to what true evangelical repentance really is. Just now some professedly Christian teachers are misleading many by saying that "repentance is only a change of mind." It is true that the original word does convey the idea of a change of mind, but the whole teaching of Scripture concerning the repentance which is not to be repented of is that it is a much more radical and complete change than is implied by our common phrase about changing one's mind. The repentance that does not include sincere sorrow for sin is not the saving Grace

"God-given repentance makes men grieve in their inmost souls over the sin they have committed – and works in them a gracious hatred of evil in every shape and form!"

that is worked by the Holy Spirit! God-given repentance makes men grieve in their inmost souls over the sin they have committed – and works in them a gracious hatred of evil in every shape and form! We cannot find a better definition of repentance than the one many of us learned at our mother's knee –

"Repentance is to leave
The sin we loved before
And show that we in earnest grieve
By doing so no more."[98]

The great 19th-century preacher, Dwight L. Moody, who needs no introduction, defined repentance as a turning away from a sinful life:

Man is born with his face turned away from God. When he truly repents, he is turned right round toward God; he leaves his old life.[99]

B. H. Carroll, the great Baptist theologian and preacher of the late 1800s was a staunch defender of fundamentalism and truth. His fierce support of the doctrine of repentance cannot be overlooked:

The preacher who leaves out repentance commits as grave a sin as the one who leaves out faith. I mean he must preach repentance just as often, and with as much emphasis, and to as many people as he preaches faith. To omit repentance, to ignore it, to depreciate it, is rebellion and treason.[100]

He went on to conclude that it was the lack of repentance that was at that very moment raising up a generation of carnal imposters in the pews, unregenerate tares among wheat:

When true repentance was preached and emphasized, there were not so many nominal professors of religion. To leave out or minimize repentance, no matter what sort of a faith you preach, is to prepare a generation of professors who are such in name only. I give it as my deliberate conviction, founded on twenty-five years of ministerial observation, that the Christian profession of today owes its lack of vital godliness, its want of practical piety, its absence from the prayer meeting, its miserable semblance of missionary life, very largely to the fact that old-fashioned repentance is so little preached. You can't put a big house on a little foundation. And no small part of such preaching comes from a class of modern evangelists who desiring more for their own glory to count a great number of converts than to lay deep foundations, reduce the conditions of salvation by one-half and make the other half but some intellectual trick of the mind rather than a radical spiritual change of the heart. Like Simon Magus, they believe indeed, but "their heart not being right in the sight of God, they have no part nor lot in this matter. They are yet in the gall of bitterness and in the bond of iniquity." Such converts know but little and care less about a system of doctrine. They are prayerless, lifeless, and to all steady church work reprobate.[101]

We have already reviewed numerous statements of faith from past centuries in Chapter 1. Among those statements, we have such clear witnesses in statements like, "Unfeigned Repentance, is an inward and true sorrow of heart for Sin,"[102] or "being deeply convinced of our guilt...we turn to God with unfeigned contrition, confession and supplication for mercy,"[103] or "Repentance is a turning from a life of self and sin to a life of submission and obedience to God's will."[104] Therefore, let us proceed to more recent history and examine some of the preachers of the century directly preceding our own.

In the 1930s and 1940s, a great soul winner and Baptist pastor, and editor of the *Baptist Standard*, J. Frank Norris, came to prominence in the southern United States. His beliefs about salvation were clear:

Baptists preach the gospel of repentance from sin.[105]

Jesus said, "Except ye repent, ye shall all likewise perish." There is the one truth that saves a man from hell – repentance.

Men don't go to hell because of their sins, but because they don't repent of their sins.[106]

In his book, *What Fundamental Baptists Believe*, Norris added this poignant indictment:

> The proper evidence [of the new birth] appears in the holy fruits of repentance and faith and newness of life…There was a time when the ministers never preached without giving a call for repentance. But it is out of date now. Oh, for a voice of a John the Baptist, "Repent ye, Repent ye, Repent ye, Repent ye!" Jesus said, "Except ye repent ye shall all likewise perish." Paul preached repentance toward God and faith toward the Lord Jesus Christ. We believe that repentance and faith are solemn obligations, and also inseparable graces, wrought in our souls by the quickening Spirit of God; thereby, being deeply convicted of our guilt, danger and helplessness, and of the way of salvation by Christ, we turn to God with unfeigned contrition, confession and supplication for mercy; at the same time heartily receiving the Lord Jesus Christ and openly confessing Him as our only and all-sufficient Saviour (sic).[107]

Contemporary with J. Frank Norris in the mid-1900s was the Canadian evangelist and pastor, Oswald J. Smith in Toronto. His evangelistic fervor saw thousands converted, and yet he eschewed *easy believism* and articulated a pro-repentance stance quite boldly. Notice his reference to humanism creeping into evangelism and the church during this period:

> Where there is genuine conviction of sin it is not necessary to urge, coax or press in the energy of the flesh; sinners will come without being forced; they will come because they must…If we are to get Holy Spirit Fruit, God must prepare the ground; the Holy Spirit must convict of sin before men can truly believe. It is right to tell people to believe when God has done His work in their hearts, but first they must feel their need. Let us wait until the Spirit of God has done

His part before we say: "believe on the Lord Jesus Christ and thou shalt be saved." Let us first see the signs of conviction... There is another Gospel, too popular in the present day, which seems to exclude conviction of sin and repentance from the scheme of Salvation; which demands from the sinner a mere intellectual assent to the fact of his guilt and sinfulness, and a like intellectual assent to the fact and sufficiency of Christ's atonement; and such assent yielded, tells him to go in peace, and to be happy in the assurance that the Lord Jesus has made it all right between his soul and God; thus crying peace, peace, when there is no peace. Flimsy and false conversions of this sort may be one reason why so many who assume the Christian profession dishonour God and bring reproach on the church by their inconsistent lives, and by their ultimate relapses into worldliness and sin...it is one thing to hold up the hand and sign a decision card, but it is quite another thing to get saved...It is one thing to have hundreds of professed converts during the excitement of the campaign, but it is another thing to come back five years after and find them still there.[108]

> *"...the Holy Spirit must convict of sin before men can truly believe."*

In the mid-1900s, B. R. Lakin was one of the most sought-after fundamentalist preachers in the US, yet he began his ministry as a humble circuit-riding preacher. In his 1964 work, *Prepare to Meet Thy God,* he described repentance in what some today would consider extreme terms:

> Repentance toward God – that's turning away from all your sin and everything you know to be wrong, and turning right about face, then trusting Jesus Christ as your complete Redeemer.[109]

G. Beauchamp Vick was a prominent pastor, author, and evangelist in the mid-1900s. He served as President of the World

Fundamental Baptist Missionary Fellowship, President of the Bible Baptist Seminary, President of Baptist Bible College, founder of the Baptist Bible Fellowship, leading figure in the Fundamental Baptist Congresses, and the pastor of Temple Baptist Church in Detroit, Michigan.[110] In the second volume of his encyclopedia on historical Baptist doctrine, *The Biblical Faith of Baptists*, Vick makes it clear that Baptists have historically (and biblically) believed repentance in the gospel means to turn from sin:

> The very moment that soul that is dead, cut off, alienated from the very life of God, sees himself as a hopeless, helpless, Hell-deserving, and Hell-bound sinner; when that soul sees that Jesus Christ is the only Way, the only hope, and when he looks away from self; when he repents of his sin and looks to the finished work of the crucified, buried and risen Lord for salvation – that very moment, instantaneously, the Spirit of God operates.[111]

John R. Rice was the founding editor of the fundamentalist periodical, *Sword of the Lord*, and a renowned Baptist pastor. His memory has since been somewhat co-opted by the antinomian movement, as his successors quickly turned against repentance. Nevertheless, there can be no doubt as to Rice's position on this important doctrine:

> To repent literally means to have a change of mind or spirit toward God and toward sin. It means to turn from your sins, earnestly, with all your heart, and trust in Jesus Christ to save you. You can see, then, how the man who believes in Christ repents and the man who repents believes in Christ. The jailer repented when he turned from sin to believe in the Lord Jesus Christ.[112]

He adds in an issue of *Sword of the Lord* this simple and uncompromising definition of gospel repentance:

> What do I mean by repent? I mean to turn your heart from
> your sin. Turn from sin in your heart and start out to live
> for God...a penitent heart that turns from your sin and turns
> to Jesus.[113]

In his book, *Dr. Rice, Here Are More Questions, Volume II*, Rice once again defines repentance scripturally in no uncertain terms as late as 1973:

> There ought to be plain preaching against sin. People ought
> to be taught to turn from sin in genuine repentance.[114]

Many in the fundamentalist movement are familiar with Harold Sightler, the prolific evangelist and founding pastor of Tabernacle Baptist Church. In his 1963 work, *Chastening and Repentance*, Sightler concluded that those who do not repent of their sins are not regenerated saints, but merely professors:

> Recognizing his guilt, there is a turning from sin. There is
> a turning to God. The actual word "repentance" means a
> turning completely around: a change of course; a change of
> mind...To think of repentance that does not cause the sinner
> to turn gladly from his sins is impossible...I know that we
> have a shallow religious movement in our times that will
> allow men to profess faith in Christ and at the same time
> continue to live in the world. Such a shallow religious faith
> is not real. These are mere professors and have no part with
> God in salvation.[115]

Another highly revered figure from the previous century, Oliver B. Greene was a renowned independent Baptist preacher, author (with over 100 printed works to his name), and the founder of the radio preaching ministry, *The Gospel Hour*.[116] In his *Commentary of Acts of the Apostles*, Greene defined saving repentance as turning from sin in this powerful excerpt:

True repentance is sorrow for sin committed against a holy God and not only sorrow for sin, but turning from sin, forsaking sin and turning to God. Sin nailed the Savior to the cross and certainly that fact alone is sufficient reason why all who have genuinely repented hate sin and forsake sinful ways.[117]

"To think of repentance that does not cause the sinner to turn gladly from his sins is impossible."

Bruce Lackey was the Dean of the Bible College at Tennessee Temple in the 1960s and 1970s as well as a professor of the Greek language. He was a stalwart defender of the *King James* translation of the Bible, an honored Baptist pastor, a traveling speaker, and an accomplished author.[118] In his book, *Repentance Is More Than a Change of Mind,* Lackey provided, in his educated view, a nutshell appraisal of repentance as traditionally held by Christianity:

> The Greek words [for repentance] mean "a change of mind which results in a change of action." When that refers to man, there is a sorrow for sin involved. This definition is substantiated both by the scholarship of Trench and Thayer, as well as by the New Testament usage.[119]

One of the greatest men of God of the previous century who stood for righteousness, holiness, old-fashioned religion, and the fundamentals of the faith would have to be Lester Roloff. A man who practiced what he preached, Roloff was highly disciplined, compassionate, zealous for good works, and busy about the Lord's business. He was most known for his radio ministry and evangelistic girls homes, but he also pastored for many years and traveled as a Baptist evangelist.[120] In his 1965 sermon, *Repent or Perish*, this modern-day prophet of God sounded out the cry for repentance in the face of compromise by his peers (of whom Jack Hyles was one):

Repentance is a godly sorrow for sin. Repentance is a forsaking of sin. Real repentance is putting your trust in Jesus Christ so you will not live like that anymore. Repentance is permanent. It is a lifelong and an eternity-long experience. You will never love the devil again once you repent. You will never flirt with the devil as the habit of your life again once you get saved. You will never be happy living in sin; it will never satisfy; and the husks of the world will never fill your longing and hungering in your soul. Repentance is something a lot bigger than a lot of people think. It is absolutely essential if you go to heaven.[121]

In no uncertain terms, Roloff drove home the point that the sinner cannot be reconciled to God with the dagger of rebellion still clutched in his fist. He firmly taught, as had his forbears, that grace cannot be granted without repentance from sin on the part of the sinner and that true repentance produces a changed life:

> *"Repentance is a godly sorrow for sin. Repentance is a forsaking of sin. Real repentance is putting your trust in Jesus Christ so you will not live like that anymore."*

I believe we ought to make right what we can make right. What if I was staying with a group of preachers and one of them stole my wallet while I was sleeping? The next day he comes up to me and tells me he is terribly sorry and asks me to forgive him. I would be glad to hear that he is sorry for stealing my wallet, but I would certainly want and expect more than that from a repentant thief. I would want my wallet back! I don't believe he has really repented unless he brings my billfold back. I don't believe you have repented until you get right and say, "Lord, I'm going to live different from now on," and by the grace of God you will live different.[122]

These and many other gospel preachers – from Martin Luther to Charles Spurgeon to John R. Rice and Lester Roloff – have confirmed both the biblical significance and the definition of repentance in the gospel. Having received God's true gospel thousands of years ago, the saints have maintained and defended this teaching through the years, passing it from generation to generation. Their voices declare in unison and clarity: without repentance from sin, there is no grace or forgiveness. This cloud of witnesses must not be ignored, discounted, or mistaken. Instead, skeptics should ask, just what did these great men of God see in the Scriptures that led them to these beliefs? Just what in the Bible has brought these many witnesses to these conclusions? What indeed?

Chapter 4

REPENTANCE IN
THE GOSPEL

And that repentance and remission of sins should be preached in his name among all nations, beginning at Jerusalem.

Luke 24:47

Over the course of the next several chapters, it will be demonstrated conclusively that the gospel of the Bible includes repentance from sin and turns a sinner onto the path of righteousness. And the first step we must take toward this end is to prove beyond any reasonable doubt that the Bible commands us to preach repentance. Before dealing with the proper definition of this word, it must be amply demonstrated that the gospel call includes an undeniable call to repent. The reader may insist that repentance means only to turn from unbelief to belief, but this is entirely beside the point of this particular chapter and will be dealt with thoroughly in Chapter 5. For now, we shall address just what the Bible says about the use of the word, repent, when dealing with the gospel and salvation.

Repentance Phobia

There are many Antinomians who will grant us the use of this word in the gospel, and there are even some who use it, themselves. They may redefine the word, but they can at least either use it or tolerate the use of it in giving the gospel call to a sinner. Yet, because the Antinomian fundamentally disregards God's law and underemphasizes holiness, he often exemplifies an aversion to the doctrine of repentance on such a level that he cannot even stand the term, itself. Indeed, there are many Antinomians who will urge you not to even use the word. In discussing the issue of repentance, they will ask you if you could give the gospel without using the word, as though they think the gospel preacher is somehow hindered by its use. Because they know in their spirit what the word truly means, they would rather be rid of it entirely.

For example, Joseph Dearing recently published an e-book on the subject featuring a forward by prominent preacher and author in the fundamentalist Baptist movement, Dr. Sam Gipp. In the e-book, Dearing argues for the antinomian position that "repentance" merely means to turn from unbelief to belief. Yet even redefining this word as he does, it still apparently turns him off, and he recommends not even using it:

> Soul-winners and tract authors need not use the word "repent" at all. It has been pointed out that the word "repent" does not appear anywhere in the book of John.[123]

It is not enough that he removes the responsibility of turning from sin from the definition of this word. It is not enough that this word is a biblical word. It is not enough that this word was used by most of the great preachers of the Bible. To Dearing, it would be better that we just not even bother with it when preaching the gospel. He goes on to say:

Because they know in their spirit what the word truly means, they would rather be rid of it entirely.

When I got saved, I had no idea what "repentance" was, and the word "repent" never entered my mind.[124]

For many Antinomians, the primary reason they offer for wanting to stay away from this word is only because it might cause confusion for the hearer. They seem to be concerned that the hearer might not be privy to their private interpretation of the word and might conclude it means turning from sin (since this is the biblical use of the term in many cases). They insist that the word might be interpreted by different listeners in many different ways, and some might be led to a works-based understanding of the gospel. Is this a valid objection? Should we play along with the Antinomian and eliminate this word from our collective vocabulary lest it confuse those more familiar with its perverted definitions than its biblical definition?

Henry A. "Harry" Ironside, the celebrated theologian, preacher, and author once dubbed "the Archbishop of Fundamentalism,"[125] wrote about this very aversion to the word, *repent*, in his 1937 book, *Except Ye Repent*. While he grants that it is not entirely necessary to always use the word and that there is certainly the possibility that it might be misunderstood from time to time, he goes on to conclude:

> But, on the other hand, it is not wise to be too squeamish about the use of an expression which we have seen to be eminently scriptural, and which the Holy Spirit Himself has used in all dispensations...what Biblical expression is there that has not been perverted in the interest of some false system throughout the so-called Christian centuries? Such words as regeneration, justification, sanctification, yes, and even the very word salvation itself, have all been grievously misused and the most unscriptural doctrines have been built upon them. Are we therefore to discard the terms themselves, or shall we not rather seek to present them in a right way, clarifying their meaning so far as we possibly can, in order that wrong conclusions may be averted?[126]

Another author to demonstrate this aversion to the term, *repentance*, was J. Dwight Pentecost, a noted *Dispensationalist* and Distinguished Professor of Bible Exposition, Emeritus, at Dallas Theological Seminary.[127]   However, he represents the strain of Antinomians who take it even a step farther and conclude that the Bible does not even teach that repentance (of any definition) is required for salvation.   In his book, *Things Which Become Sound Doctrine*, Pentecost states brazenly:

> Repentance is not a prerequisite to salvation; for if repentance is required, salvation is based, at least in part on works...We should suggest to you from the Word of God that repentance is included in believing. It is not a separate act which conditions salvation, but rather it is included in the act of believing.[128]

What Pentecost is doing is claiming that "repentance" is not required for salvation because it is the same thing as believing. On one hand, he acknowledges repentance is turning from sin when he alleges this is adding works to the gospel. But in the very next breath, he pretends the word only means to turn from unbelief to belief. And if repentance is the exact same thing as believing, it is therefore redundant and unnecessary to mention "repentance" in the gospel. We can do without this inconvenient word (and all its connotations of turning from sin). In redefining it as believing, the Antinomian, by sleight of hand, makes repentance seemingly vanish into thin air and attempts to convince the biblically illiterate that belief is all that should stand in its place.

In their phobia of the righteous word, *repentance*, Antinomians beg us to not even use it, and some go so far as to insist that it is not even part of the gospel. They pretend it is a non-essential synonym for believing and not even part of God's plan of salvation. They ignore gospel passages and Scripture verses insisting on the absolute necessity of repentance, some of which list only repentance as a requirement for salvation. But if repentance is merely a non-essential synonym for belief, why does the Bible give the term such prominent billing in Scripture and include pivotal passages like the following?

In redefining it as believing, the Antinomian, by sleight of hand, makes repentance seemingly vanish into thin air.

I tell you, Nay: but, except ye repent, ye shall all likewise perish. Or those eighteen, upon whom the tower in Siloam fell, and slew them, think ye that they were sinners above all men that dwelt in Jerusalem? I tell you, Nay: but, except ye repent, ye shall all likewise perish.

Luke 13:3-5

But go ye and learn what that meaneth, I will have mercy, and not sacrifice: for I am not come to call the righteous, but sinners to repentance.

Matthew 9:13

From that time Jesus began to preach, and to say, Repent: for the kingdom of heaven is at hand.

Matthew 4:17

And the times of this ignorance God winked at; but now commandeth all men every where to repent:

Acts 17:30

Preconditions in the Gospel

As Pentecost's previously mentioned quote demonstrates, the Antinomian takes umbrage at the insinuation that God might require a precondition for salvation, not realizing that God's preconditions do not equate to meritorious works. Failing to make this crucial distinction between earning salvation and simply being eligible for salvation, the Antinomian fundamentally rejects the notion of repentance as a precondition, regardless of how it is defined. And yet it is apparent from Scripture that salvation is contingent upon certain prerequisites – as fundamental and obvious as some of them may be. To list a few:

- Human – the Bible never indicates non-humans are eligible for salvation.
- Physically living – the Bible tells us now is the accepted time, while we are still alive.
- Sinners – Christ did not come to call the righteous, only sinners.
- Repentant – There is no pardon to the rebel who retains his seditious intentions.
- Believing – No one can be saved who does not place belief in Christ.

Would fulfilling any of these qualifications or preconditions for salvation equate to earning salvation? Of course not. And yet, are they not all absolutely necessary before one can be saved? Obviously, a precondition or qualification is not the same as a work. Otherwise, why would Christ use such language as "except ye repent" in Luke 13? Clearly, He was listing a qualification, which the failure to meet would disqualify from eligibility.

God's preconditions do not equate to meritorious works.

And while some reject Luke 13 as applying only to a physical death, referencing the death of those who died at the tower of Siloam, we have only to ask ourselves what the point of Christ's entire ministry was (to save people from their sins[129]) to understand that He spoke not only of their physical death, but also of the spiritual death of the listener. Those who fail to make this application are in the same category as those who failed to make the same application when Christ spoke of tearing down the temple and rebuilding it as a reference to His own death and resurrection. After all, if the point of Christ's ministry was to warn about impending physical death, how can we find meaning today in the phrase, "shall not perish," found in John 3:16?

Furthermore, we can discern that Christ considered repentance a suitable precondition for forgiveness simply by paying heed to His admonition in Luke 17:

> Take heed to yourselves: If thy brother trespass against thee, rebuke him; and if he repent, forgive him. And if he trespass against thee seven times in a day, and seven times in a day turn again to thee, saying, I repent; thou shalt forgive him.[130]

Pay close attention to that small word that indicates the precondition: "if." Does Christ here indicate that we should always forgive our brother who trespasses against us? Not at all! On the contrary, He says twice that forgiveness should follow "if" the brother repents. Are we to conclude that Christ wants us to hold out for our brother to earn our forgiveness? Not at all! But it is simply common sense and the position of our Savior that the precondition for forgiveness and mercy should be repenting from the offending transgression. As Harry Ironside put it:

> Surely no sane, thoughtful reader of the record can escape the conclusion that repentance, while in no sense meritorious, is nevertheless a prerequisite to saving faith. An unrepentant man can never, in the very nature of things, lay hold of the Gospel message in appropriating faith, thus receiving the Lord Jesus as his own personal Saviour (sic). Why, then, should any preacher of the Gospel be hesitant about calling men to repentance today?[131]

It is also worth noting that repentance and faith are intermixed and inseparable in the work of regeneration. The sinner who believes has repented. The sinner who repents already has faith that he can be forgiven. The two are intertwined and married completely. Chronologically, we would be hard pressed to establish whether one comes before the other. And yet, by the same merit, without one, the other cannot be. In this sense, in the new birth, the prerequisite of repentance must be met before regenerating faith is accomplished.

Additional Witnesses

As observed by Elihu, God's messenger in the book of Job, "God speaketh once, yea twice, yet man perceiveth it not."[132] It is to the shame of believers that they often cannot be convinced by one or two admonitions in Scripture on a matter. Nevertheless, since there are numerous Bible passages that agree, if the preceding Scriptures are deemed insufficient by the reader, the following are presented as further witnesses to the truth that repentance, regardless of how we shall come to define it, is emphatically part of the gospel.

Observe the inescapable association of repentance with the gospel call in these passages:

> Now after that John was put in prison, Jesus came into Galilee, preaching the gospel of the kingdom of God, And saying, The time is fulfilled, and the kingdom of God is at hand: repent ye, and believe the gospel.
>
> Mark 1:14-15

> For godly sorrow worketh repentance to salvation not to be repented of: but the sorrow of the world worketh death.
>
> II Corinthians 7:10

> Then Peter said unto them, Repent, and be baptized every one of you in the name of Jesus Christ for the remission of sins, and ye shall receive the gift of the Holy Ghost.
>
> Acts 2:38

> Repent ye therefore, and be converted, that your sins may be blotted out, when the times of refreshing shall come from the presence of the Lord.
>
> Acts 3:19

> Thus it is written, and thus it behooved Christ to suffer, and to rise from the dead the third day: And that repentance and

remission of sins should be preached in his name among all nations, beginning at Jerusalem.

> Luke 24:46-47

Notice the Luke 24 passage, which is a rendition of the Great Commission. What better authority is there on which we can base our gospel doctrine than on the Great Commission? And here it states that repentance is part of the gospel. In fact, the disciples were commanded to preach repentance even before the crucifixion, resurrection, and subsequent Great Commission. We find Christ charging His disciples with His message, and then the Bible says of their obedience that "they went out, and preached that men should repent."[133] Paul, the great apostle to the Gentiles, echoed this command in his ministry report to the elders of the church at Ephesus:

What better authority is there on which we can base our gospel doctrine than on the Great Commission?

> And how I kept back nothing that was profitable unto you, but have shewed you, and have taught you publicly, and from house to house, Testifying both to the Jews, and also to the Greeks, repentance toward God, and faith toward our Lord Jesus Christ.
>
> Acts 20:20-21

Not only is repentance preached as part of the gospel of the disciples during and after Christ's ministry, it also preceded it in the ministry of His forerunner, John the Baptist. In fact, it is the gospel of repentance that defines the ministry of John:

> In those days came John the Baptist, preaching in the wilderness of Judaea, And saying, Repent ye: for the kingdom of heaven is at hand.
>
> Matthew 3:1-2

Incidentally, we have only to continue reading the passage to find out just what this repentance was from. Was it from unbelief? Was it from idolatry? Actually, the passage clearly tells us that John's gospel message was repentance from sin. Soon after the Bible records him calling for repentance, it records his listeners "confessing their sins."[134]

God saw fit to intimately relate repentance to the gospel in not one, not two, but many passages, so there would be no mistake on this point. We shall soon address the biblical definition of the term, but regardless of how it is defined, let no one pretend that repentance does not belong in the gospel call. Indeed, there is immense joy in heaven over sinners repenting:

> I say unto you, that likewise joy shall be in heaven over one sinner that repenteth, more than over ninety and nine just persons, which need no repentance.
> Likewise, I say unto you, there is joy in the presence of the angels of God over one sinner that repenteth.
> Luke 15:7, 10

Properly understood, this association of repentance with the gospel does not dilute the grace of God or corrupt the gospel with works. A precondition or prerequisite required for the sinner to be a candidate for grace in no way equates to meritorious works. The sinner does not earn salvation by his repentance any more than by his faith. And yet both are equally necessary for free grace to be extended to the sinner. We find this pattern reaching all the way back to the Old Covenant. Many are familiar with the system of sacrifices for temporal covering of sins in the Old Testament. The sacrifice typified the coming Lamb of God being sacrificed once for all in the New Testament. But a lesser known requirement was to accompany the trespass or sin offering:

> And it shall be, when he shall be guilty in one of these things, that **he shall confess that he hath sinned in that**

thing: And he shall bring his trespass offering unto the Lord for his sin which he hath sinned, a female from the flock, a lamb or a kid of the goats, for a sin offering; and the priest shall make an atonement for him concerning his sin (*emphasis added*).

Leviticus 5:5-6

Notice from the passage that the priest could not make atonement for the sinner unless the sin offering was accompanied first by confession of sin. This confession was not meritorious in any way, and yet God here provided for an opportunity to remove from the rebellious sinner his dagger of sin before he could be forgiven for it. The great commentator, Matthew Henry, notes this dual requirement and how this Old Testament type points to repentance in the gospel of grace:

The sinner does not earn salvation by his repentance any more than by his faith. And yet both are equally necessary for free grace to be extended to the sinner.

The offender must confess his sin and bring his offering; and the offering was not accepted unless it was accompanied with a penitential confession and a humble prayer for pardon...As the atonement was not accepted without his repentance, so his repentance would not justify him without the atonement. Thus, in our reconciliation to God, Christ's part and ours are both needful.[135]

Having established beyond any reasonable doubt that repentance is inherent within the gospel and a prerequisite for grace, we now turn to the definition of repentance. Regardless of its definition, repentance is intimately connected with the gospel and held up as a precondition for the new birth. In the chapter to follow, repentance will be defined. This term will be broken down, defined, and applied to the gospel, comparing spiritual things with spiritual,[136] building on this principle that repentance cannot be separated out from the gospel or cast aside as a mere trifle or garnish. The record shows that Christ and his disciples placed much emphasis on repentance, that it was part of the Great Commission, and that it was frequently included in the gospel call. Let there be no doubt on this point, that without repentance, there can be no salvation.

Chapter 5

REPENTANCE DEFINED

But go ye and learn what that meaneth, I will have mercy, and not sacrifice: for I am not come to call the righteous, but sinners to repentance.

Matthew 9:13

Possibly the single most deadly attack of the Antinomians in recent generations was to redefine repentance as a change from unbelief to belief. And yet, removing sin from the definition betrays their motivation. As we have established, Antinomians, then and now, generally do not esteem God's law or holiness and therefore do not view sin as a significant problem. It then follows from this philosophy that the gospel would not address such an insignificant issue as sin when, true to their humanistic bent, they see hell as the primary issue. And so repentance, which we have seen has always been about sin, now becomes just a useless synonym for faith. The treasonous rebel against God is free to bring his weapons of war to the truce table for his get-out-of-hell-free card. As long as he expresses some sort of intellectual assent or belief that Jesus died for him, he is now "saved," sins and all.

This could not be farther from the truth. In reality, the Bible defines this word quite thoroughly in its usage to mean turning from an action, whether committed or intended. This can easily be established merely by reading the Scriptures and considering the context. In the *King James Bible*, the word, *repent*, in all its variations, occurs 112 times in 105 verses. The very first mention refers to God turning from an action committed. The very last mention refers to people turning from actions they had committed. And all in between, with very few exceptions, this is what we find the term to mean. The statistics do not lie. There is absolutely no basis for the groundless theory that "repent" in Scripture means only or primarily to turn from unbelief to belief.

Though the Antinomian is quick to cry that God repents more times than anyone else mentioned in the Bible – ignoring the obvious explanation that God is also the central character and most mentioned person in the Bible overall – the point is seldom made that His repentance still refers to His turning from an action, whether committed or intended. The Antinomian thinks he has proven repentance does not mean turning from sin, because God cannot sin and He repents more than anyone – therefore it must mean turning from unbelief to belief. But they are simply ignorant of how the word is actually used in Scripture. It almost never refers to turning from or to a belief or opinion. And of the 105 verses in which the word is found, at least 50 of them refer to turning from sin specifically (48%), while the overwhelming majority refer to turning from a general action, committed or intended – which can include sinful actions – *not* a mere philosophy or just the sin of unbelief. At least 87 verses (83%) out of 105 are used in this way in Scripture. This raises the question, if a word is used a particular way in the Bible more than four-fifths of the time, why should we not agree that is how the word should be used?

I use the phrase, *at least*, when giving these statistics, because there are some passages I have placed in the "unclear" category in the interest of intellectual honesty and fairness. The numbers may, in fact, be higher than 50 verses referencing turning from sin and 87 verses referencing turning from an action. But the context for some of the verses not included in these figures is ambiguous enough that we can leave them in the "unclear" category and still make our point rather decisively. In a few cases (approximately 8%), usually when using the passive voice (e.g. "It repented him"), the term can also refer to an attitude of pity or sorrow for someone else. But of the 105 total verses, only two (2%) could safely be construed as referencing a turning from unbelief to belief, making this far and away the least

If a word is used a particular way in the Bible more than four-fifths of the time, why should we not agree that is how the word should be used?

likely definition for the word in Scripture. And in even in these two cases, it should be remembered that unbelief is a type of sin. This data is summarized in the following tables to illustrate the significant disparity between the antinomian definition of the word and our own:

Table 1: A turn from an action (typically negative) committed or intended:
87 verses

Genesis 6:6	Exodus 13:17	Exodus 32:12
Exodus 32:14	Numbers 23:19	I Samuel 15:11
I Samuel 15:29	I Samuel 15:35	II Samuel 24:16
I Kings 8:47-48	I Chronicles 21:15	Job 42:6
Psalm 106:45	Psalm 110:4	Jeremiah 4:28
Jeremiah 8:6	Jeremiah 15:6	Jeremiah 18:8
Jeremiah 18:10	Jeremiah 20:16	Jeremiah 26:3
Jeremiah 26:13	Jeremiah 26:19	Jeremiah 31:19
Jeremiah 42:10	Ezekiel 14:6	Ezekiel 18:30
Ezekiel 24:14	Hosea 11:8	Hosea 13:14
Joel 2:13	Joel 2:14	Amos 7:3
Amos 7:6	Jonah 3:9	Jonah 3:10
Jonah 4:2	Zechariah 8:14	Matthew 3:2
Matthew 3:8	Matthew 3:11	Matthew 9:13

Matthew 12:41	Matthew 21:29	Matthew 21:32
Matthew 27:3	Mark 1:4	Mark 2:17
Luke 3:3	Luke 3:8	Luke 5:32
Luke 11:32	Luke 13:3	Luke 13:5
Luke 15:7	Luke 15:10	Luke 17:3
Luke 17:4	Luke 24:47	Acts 2:38
Acts 3:19	Acts 5:31	Acts 8:22
Acts 13:24	Acts 17:30	Acts 19:4
Acts 26:20	Romans 2:4	Romans 11:29
II Corinthians 7:8	II Corinthians 7:9-10	II Corinthians 12:21
Hebrews 6:1	Hebrews 7:21	Hebrews 12:17
Revelation 2:5	Revelation 2:16	Revelation 2:21-22
Revelation 3:3	Revelation 3:19	Revelation 9:20-21
Revelation 16:9	Revelation 16:11	

Table 2: A turn from actual sin committed or intended:
50 verses

I Kings 8:47-48	Job 42:6	Jeremiah 8:6
Jeremiah 31:19	Ezekiel 14:6	Ezekiel 18:30
Matthew 3:2	Matthew 3:8	Matthew 3:11
Matthew 9:13	Matthew 12:41	Matthew 21:29
Matthew 21:32	Matthew 27:3	Mark 1:4
Mark 2:17	Luke 3:3	Luke 3:8
Luke 5:32	Luke 11:32	Luke 13:3
Luke 13:5	Luke 15:7	Luke 15:10
Luke 17:3	Luke 17:4	Luke 24:47
Acts 2:38	Acts 3:19	Acts 5:31
Acts 8:22	Acts 13:24	Acts 17:30
Acts 19:4	Acts 26:20	Romans 2:4
II Corinthians 7:9-10	II Corinthians 12:21	Revelation 2:5
Revelation 2:16	Revelation 2:21-22	Revelation 3:3

Revelation 3:19	Revelation 9:20-21	Revelation 16:9
Revelation 16:11		

Table 3: A turn from unbelief to belief:
2 verses

Luke 16:30	II Timothy 2:25

Table 4: Sorrow, sympathy, pity, or regret for someone else:
8 verses

Deuteronomy 32:36	Judges 2:18	Judges 21:6
Judges 21:15	Psalm 90:13	Psalm 106:45
Psalm 135:14	Hosea 11:8	

Table 5: Definition not explicit from text:
11 verses

Matthew 4:17	Matthew 9:13	Matthew 11:21
Matthew 21:32	Mark 1:15	Mark 6:12
Luke 10:13	Acts 11:18	Acts 20:21
Hebrews 6:6	II Peter 3:9	

This information reflects the author's prayerful and careful study of each passage within its immediate context. But the reader is invited to carefully consider the verdict of each specific passage and see for themselves that this data is verifiably accurate. Each passage is listed along with a comment of classification in Appendix A. There can be no doubt that, if we truly are Bible believers, and if we truly allow the Bible to define its terms, the definition is quite simple to nail down. More than four times out of five in Scripture, it means a turn of the heart or mind from actions committed or intended.

Repentance Described in Scripture

It is the contention of this book that repentance must be from sin in order for God to administer saving grace to the sinner. Repentance merely from unbelief is incomplete and an impossibility when it comes to the gospel. But what about the word useage in any context? Does repentance, even outside of the context of the gospel, mean to turn from sin? Building on the overwhelming case for the Bible's definition of repentance as turning from an action in general, let us examine some of these passages in more detail to more fully grasp the terms in which God describes repentance as a turn from sin specifically. In so doing, we shall establish beyond a shadow of a doubt that when men repent, it usually refers to turning from sin, regardless of the context. Take, for example, the following Old Testament passage:

When men repent, it usually refers to turning from sin, regardless of the context.

> Therefore I will judge you, O house of Israel, every one according to his ways, saith the Lord God. Repent, and turn yourselves from all your transgressions; so iniquity shall not be your ruin.
> Cast away from you all your transgressions, whereby ye have transgressed; and make you a new heart and a new spirit: for why will ye die, O house of Israel?
> For I have no pleasure in the death of him that dieth, saith the Lord God: wherefore turn yourselves, and live ye.
> Ezekiel 18:30-32

In this passage, we see quite clearly that God, speaking in parallel phrases to reinforce the meaning, tells the house of Israel to "Repent, and turn yourselves." But He does not stop there. Turn yourselves from what? From "all your transgressions." The next verse tells them again to "Cast away from you all your transgressions," and the verse following concludes with, "turn yourselves."

The Antinomian is quick to point out the phrase, "Why will ye die," to argue that this is not referring to salvation, but merely physical life and death. Yet this is entirely beside the point. Because at this time, we are only concerned with the general use of the term in any context, salvation or otherwise. The pertinent point is, in this passage – as in most passages dealing with mankind – it is obvious that *repent* means to turn from transgressions or sins. Likewise, just a few chapters prior, God issues a very similar warning:

> Therefore say unto the house of Israel, Thus saith the Lord God; Repent, and turn yourselves from your idols; and turn away your faces from all your abominations.
>
> Ezekiel 14:6

When the Antinomian sees anything about idols in a verse with repentance, he immediately jumps on it. This is his opportunity to reinforce the notion that repentance only means to turn away from unbelief (or false belief, in the case of idolatry) to belief in Jesus. Yet four things should be observed by way of rebuttal:

1. First, idolatry is still an action and is, therefore, consistent with the prevailing definition we have uncovered from Scripture.
2. Idolatry is a sin, and so repentance in this context still refers to turning from sin.
3. We are not even discussing the gospel at this time – this will be discussed in the next chapter. For the purposes of this chapter, we are simply showing that repentance typically means to turn from sin, regardless of whether in the context of the gospel or not.

4. Finally, the text goes on to add, "and turn…from all your abominations." So in this passage, repentance means to turn not only from the sin of idolatry, but from *all* sin.

Another passage that clearly demonstrates repentance is typically from sin is found in II Corinthians. And this passage actually provides a list of sins to be repented of or turned from:

> And lest, when I come again, my God will humble me among you, and that I shall bewail many which have sinned already, and have not repented of the uncleanness and fornication and lasciviousness which they have committed.
>
> II Corinthians 12:21

In Acts 3, the Bible tells sinners to repent because of their sins and then, a few verses later, spells it out as a turn from iniquities:

> Repent ye therefore, and be converted, that your sins may be blotted out, when the times of refreshing shall come from the presence of the Lord.
> Unto you first God, having raised up his Son Jesus, sent him to bless you, in turning away every one of you from his iniquities.
>
> Acts 3:19, 26

In Luke, Jesus speaks of one man sinning against another man, once again describing repentance as turning from sin or trespass:

> Take heed to yourselves: If thy brother trespass against thee, rebuke him; and if he repent, forgive him.
> And if he trespass against thee seven times in a day, and seven times in a day turn again to thee, saying, I repent; thou shalt forgive him.
>
> Luke 17:3-4

In Revelation 2, repentance is described as turning from the sins of fornication and adultery:

> And I gave her space to repent of her fornication; and she repented not.
> Behold, I will cast her into a bed, and them that commit adultery with her into great tribulation, except they repent of their deeds.
>
> Revelation 2:21-22

A few chapters later, we have yet another description of repentance with vivid details telling us repentance involves turning from sinful "works:"

> And the rest of the men which were not killed by these plagues yet repented not of the works of their hands, that they should not worship devils, and idols of gold, and silver, and brass, and stone, and of wood: which neither can see, nor hear, nor walk:
>
> Revelation 9:20

Once again, we can almost sense the Antinomian honing in on words like "devils" and "idols." And it might be tempting to conclude that this passage is only referring to repenting from idolatry, which, as we have already seen, is still a sin and an action ("works of their hands"), and thus consistent with our biblical definition. But it is also not the end of the statement. Notice the colon mark at the end of the verse, denoting a list is about to expound on the theme:

> Neither repented they of their murders, nor of their sorceries, nor of their fornication, nor of their thefts.
>
> Revelation 9:21

Later in the same book, we have the record of God spilling out His wrath on the kingdom of the Beast, a kingdom defined by its rebellion against God and allegiance to Satan. And yet, it is not the fact that this kingdom had the wrong allegiance for which the text records God's wrath being poured out. That would have seemed the obvious choice, and yet, the text says it was the things they *did* – in other words, it was their sinful actions:

> And the fifth angel poured out his vial upon the seat of the beast; and his kingdom was full of darkness; and they gnawed their tongues for pain,
> And blasphemed the God of heaven because of their pains and their sores, and repented not of their deeds.
> Revelation 16:10-11

In Acts, we read of Simon the Sorcerer, who wanted to buy the power of God with money. When Peter rebuked him for it, he used the word, "repent," telling him he needed God's forgiveness for having intended to buy the power of God. The word is clearly used here to describe someone turning away from a sinful and wicked act they intended to commit:

> But Peter said unto him, Thy money perish with thee, because thou hast thought that the gift of God may be purchased with money.
> Thou hast neither part nor lot in this matter: for thy heart is not right in the sight of God.
> Repent therefore of this thy wickedness, and pray God, if perhaps the thought of thine heart may be forgiven thee.
> For I perceive that thou art in the gall of bitterness, and in the bond of iniquity.
> Acts 8:20-23

This passage demonstrates the other part of our definition of repentance – that it is not only for actions committed, but also actions intended. Repentance is to utterly abhor sin, to turn away from it, and to see it through God's holy eyes as repugnant and impossible to live with. This surrender and transformation is precisely what Paul spoke about in his description of repentance when he stated that his mission was:

> To open their eyes, and to turn them from the power of Satan unto God, that they may receive forgiveness of sins, and inheritance among them which are sanctified by faith... that they should repent and turn to God, and do works meet for repentance.
>
> Acts 26:18-20

The great 18th-century commentator, Matthew Henry, spoke of this reorientation contained in repentance in his commentary on this passage:

> To repent of their sins, to be sorry for them and to confess them, and enter into covenant against them...to change their mind and change their way, and undo what they had done amiss...they must come into conformity to God – must not only turn from that which is evil, but turn to that which is good...this is that which is required from the whole revolted degenerate race of mankind...turn our eye to him, turn our heart to him, and turn our feet to his testimonies.[137]

And so repentance involves ending mankind's revolt on a personal, individual level, changing both the mind and the way, and turning away from sinful actions to God. It is entering into a truce with God, a "covenant against" sinful actions or intentions. It is being enlightened to see the darkness of sin and the light of holiness. This is how the word, *repentance*, is to be understood. This

Repentance is to utterly abhor sin, to turn away from it, and to see it through God's holy eyes as repugnant and impossible to live with.

is how repentance is defined and described in Scripture. And what is more, this is consistent with the heritage passed down to us by our spiritual forebears. Indeed, 19th century Baptist pastor and preeminent historian, Isaac Backus, wrote in his authoritative chronology of the church in pre-US America that it was this understanding of repentance as a turning from sin to God that united the colonial Baptists as a people during the 1700s. He stated:

> Many ruin their souls by fighting against God, but it is impossible for him to be deceived or disappointed of his designs of mercy, as well as of justice. And free salvation by the Son of God is held forth to all men...and the condemnation of all who do not receive him, is because they hate the light. John III 14-20. Therefore the most moving methods ought to be taken with sinners in general, to enlighten and turn them from sin to God. Light concerning these things gained gradually among the Baptists in Virginia, so as to unite them as one people in 1787, and they have increased much since.[138]

This and many other witnesses previously mentioned confirm what we have already seen from Scripture. As we have seen in the previous chapter that repentance is required in the gospel regardless of definition, so we have proven in this chapter that repentance is typically defined as turning from an action regardless of context. Let it be stated again fully and completely: repentance is a change of mind and heart for actions, committed or intended, resulting in a change of course.

What Repentance Is Not

There often persists some confusion as to just what repentance is, even after explaining it as we have done. In the interest of preventing undue controversy about this doctrine and what all it entails, it would be profitable to disavow certain misconceptions and thus examine what repentance is not just as we have examined what it is. And so, in the interest of distinguishing biblical repentance from works salvation, let us consider those things sometimes confused with repentance.

- Repentance is not *penance*: Though Roman Catholic translations of the Bible often translate it as "do penance,"[139] repentance is not the same as the sacramental duty of getting sins absolved by ritual or restitution. Nothing man does can ever atone for his own sin. To attempt self-payment is futile.
- Repentance is not *reformation*: Though the first objection to preaching repentance from sin in the gospel is that this adds works to the gospel (this objection will be dealt with in detail in Chapter 8), it often comes down to semantics. The objector is confusing repentance with reformation, turning over a new leaf, cleaning up one's life, etc. Yet this is not at all what we mean by repentance. Sinful man can never impress God with his righteousness, which is filthy in God's sight.[140]
- Repentance is not mere *confession*: Though repentance can sometimes include confessing sins, just as it can sometimes include tears or kneeling, these things do not define repentance. Confession in the Roman Catholic sense of reading off a list of sins is not at all what we mean by repentance.
- Repentance is not mere *penitence*: Penitence is primarily identified as sorrow for sin. And while biblical repentance certainly includes penitence or sorrow for sin, this is not all it entails. The objection against repentance in the gospel that Judas was sorry for his sin and yet died and went to hell is a valid one. Mere sorrow is not repentance. Repentance includes godly sorrow, but is not limited to it.

If these things are what is meant by repentance, then of course it is fitting to reject the notion that repentance must precede salvation. And yet, if true repentance is wrought by the Holy Ghost in the heart of the convicted sinner before salvation, these elements will undoubtedly follow after salvation and be characteristic of someone who has experienced the new birth.

True Repentance vs. False Repentance

True repentance is a miraculous work of the Holy Ghost that can hardly be itemized and discussed in technical terms without obscuring the elegance and mystery of it to some degree. Nevertheless, we should not oversimplify this doctrine, as some do who may not hold to the extreme antinomian view yet still fall short of fully grasping this important biblical doctrine. Some who claim to have repented and been saved later fall away from grace, leading us to conclude that they never truly grasped repentance to begin with. And so, we must differentiate true repentance from false repentance.

Far from promoting dependence on good works to save, the doctrine of repentance actually teaches that nothing man does is sufficient – that both rebellion and self-righteousness are futile. The sinner who comes to a saving repentance recognizes the utter insufficiency of all his devices to correct his situation. Up to that point, he might have tried to strike a bargain with God or get on His good side. But in true repentance, there is no more guile or disguises, just guilt. Only total admission of the sinner's depravity and futility and his unconditional surrender to God's terms can make a child of the devil a candidate for grace. We sense this sentiment in Job's statement of surrender:

> I have heard of thee by the hearing of the ear: but now mine eye seeth thee. Wherefore I abhor myself, and repent in dust and ashes.[141]

Job no longer saw himself through his own eyes, but through God's. Likewise, he no longer saw God through his own eyes, but God's. At the point of repentance, the sinner no longer sees himself as a good person. He no longer sees God as just the man upstairs. He perceives his sin as exceeding sinful and God as infinitely holy. He now recognizes the utter futility of bargaining with God or continuing in his sin. Repentance is agreement with God, or as Paris Reidhead put it in the exceptional sermon, *Ten Shekels and a Shirt*:

> But I believe that the only ones whom God actually witnesses by His Spirit and are born of Him are the people, whether they say it or not, that come to Jesus Christ and say something like this, "Lord Jesus, I'm going to obey you and love you and serve you and do what you want me to do as long as I live, even if I go to hell at the end of the road, simply because you are worthy to be loved and obeyed and served, and I'm not trying to make a deal with you!" Do you see the difference? Do you see the difference - between a Levite serving for ten shekels and a shirt, or a Micah building a chapel because God will do you good, and someone that repents for the glory of God?[142]

How different this description is from the halfway definitions some use for repentance! Does this sound like the sorrow of Judas, who was indeed sorry, and yet hung himself in despair? Of course not. Because repentance is not merely being sorry for your sin. Indeed, his regret and remorse was just as humanistic as the Antinomian's refusal to repent. Like the Antinomian who sees the gospel as a solution to prevent him from going to hell rather than to pay for the sins he committed against a holy God, Judas sorrowed only for himself and not for God. As Harry Ironside points out, Judas only saw the whole situation through his own eyes:

"Lord Jesus, I'm going to obey you and love you and serve you and do what you want me to do as long as I live, even if I go to hell at the end of the road, simply because you are worthy to be loved and obeyed and served."

Though the victim of a remorse that must become increasingly poignant as the eons roll on, his must ever be a hopeless repentance because it is based, not on the sense of the wrong done to God, but of the wretchedness in which he involved himself by his stupendous folly.[143]

Paul wrote to the Corinthians about this difference between humanistic – or worldly – sorrow and godly sorrow. He pointed out that godly sorrow entails an entirely new perspective and attitude:

For godly sorrow worketh repentance to salvation not to be repented of: but the sorrow of the world worketh death. For behold this selfsame thing, that ye sorrowed after a godly sort, what carefulness it wrought in you, yea, what clearing of yourselves, yea, what indignation, yea, what fear, yea, what vehement desire, yea, what zeal, yea, what revenge! In all things ye have approved yourselves to be clear in this matter.

II Corinthians 7:10-11

Some believe repentance to be the acknowledgment, confession, and condemnation of their sin in addition to their sorrowing over it. But this is still not quite enough to be considered true repentance in and of itself. In I Samuel 24, King Saul penitently acknowledges his sinfulness in pursuing David and seeking to kill him. He cries out against the sin and even seems to sorrow over it, and yet we find him once again seeking to kill David just two chapters later. In Exodus, Pharaoh responded to the plague of hail with a clear acknowledgment of his sin. He stated, "I have sinned," going so far as to add, "the LORD is righteous, and I and my people are wicked."[144] We have no reason to doubt his sincerity. And yet, before the end of the chapter, Pharaoh was back to his old

Clearly, admitting to God that you are a sinner does not rise to the level of biblical repentance.

ways. Clearly, admitting to God that you are a sinner does not rise to the level of biblical repentance.

True repentance is not even to be found in calling out to God for mercy. Any lost person can want mercy and ask God for it without being saved. In I Kings 8, King Solomon prays to God on behalf of his people, acknowledging their sin, and asking God to forgive them and spare them from judgment. But he does not stop there. Solomon asks God these things conditioned on certain terms, one of which being that this people "shall turn again to thee."[145] Matthew Henry comments on this passage:

> That the condition of the removal of the judgment was something more than barely praying for it. He could not, he would not, ask that their prayer might be answered unless they did also turn from their sin (v. 35) and turn to God (v. 33), that is, unless they did truly repent and reform. On no other terms may we look for salvation in this world or the other.[146]

Some believe the sinner must only repent of being a sinner – in other words, of being born of Adam with an Adamic nature. Renowned dispensationalist author and pastor, Peter S. Ruckman, for example, taught that "evangelical repentance is being sorry for what you are."[147] They believe in repentance, but only in repenting of something the sinner really had no choice in. But this is not what the Bible says of true repentance. While the sinner who is granted true repentance by the Holy Ghost may repent of anything and everything he can think of, including being born into sin, chances are he won't. And he does not need to. Nowhere does the Bible require the sinner to make a list of all sins committed and repent of them, but it does tell the sinner to repent of the sins, themselves, as opposed to the nature. We find the Bible commanding sinners to repent of their deeds, iniquities, abominations, works, etc. – but nowhere to repent of being born with a sin nature.

True repentance, as opposed to these false or insufficient impressions of it, entails at least three elements, if we must itemize so mysterious a supernatural gift. We have seen how William Tyndale, the great martyr and Bible translator, described repentance as containing four primary elements: confession, contrition, faith, and satisfaction. The fourth element, satisfaction, refers to those works that follow saving repentance which the Bible calls "fruits meet for repentance."[148] Tyndale could not have been more accurate in describing true repentance when discussing the first three elements, which come prior to salvation, and the fourth, which comes after:

> Which conversion or turning, if it be unfeigned, these four do accompany it and are included therein: Confession, not in the priest's ear, for that is but man's invention, but to God in the heart, and before all the congregation of God; how that we be sinners and sinful, and that our whole nature is corrupt, and inclined to sin and all unrighteousness, and therefore evil, wicked, and damnable; and his Law holy and just, by which our sinful nature is rebuked: and also to our neighbours (sic), if we have offended any person particularly. Then Contrition, sorrowfulness that we be such damnable sinners, and not only have sinned but are wholly inclined to sin still. Thirdly, Faith (of which our old doctors have made no mention at all in the description of their penance), that God for Christ's sake doth forgive us, and receive us to mercy, and is at one with us, and will heal our corrupt nature. And fourthly, Satisfaction, or amends-making, not to God with holy works, but to my neighbor whom I have hurt, and to the congregation of God, whom I have offended, (if any open crime be found in me); and submitting of a man's self unto the congregation or church of Christ, and to the officers of the same, to have his life corrected and governed henceforth of them.[149]

Notice Tyndale differentiates confession from the Roman Catholic version, as a complete abhorrence and admission of sin and guilt, rather than a ritualistic recitation. We find this in the converts of

John the Baptist, "confessing their sins" upon hearing his message of repentance.[150] We find this in the wisdom of Proverbs, which tells us minimizing sins will not work, "but whoso confesseth and forsaketh them shall have mercy."[151] In his classic story of Christian's journey to the Celestial City, *Pilgrim's Progress*, John Bunyan records a conversation between fellow traveler, Faithful, and a vain professor, named Talkative. Their conversation hits on the difference between ritualistic confession or condemnation of sin and true, saving hatred for sin. Faithful asks Talkative how grace first appears in the heart of man, to which Talkative responds, "it causeth there a great outcry against sin." Surprisingly, this is not good enough for Faithful, the true believer, whose response emphasizes the need for utter abhorrence of sin:

> A man may cry out against sin of policy; but he cannot abhor it but by virtue of a godly antipathy against it. I have heard many cry out against sin in the pulpit, who yet can abide it well enough in the heart, house, and conversation. Joseph's mistress cried out with a loud voice, as if she had been very chaste; but she would willingly, notwithstanding that, have committed uncleanness with him.[152]

Next, Tyndale tells us that contrition is part of true repentance. Contrition is a far stronger word than mere sorrow, and encapsulates that which the Bible sometimes refers to as "godly sorrow." Ironside tells us of godly sorrow that it is "produced by the Spirit of God" and not to be confused with worldly sorrow, "which is simply remorse because of the dire consequences following upon evil ways."[153] It involves brokenness and surrender. This is the kind of sorrow that gets God's attention.

> The LORD is nigh unto them that are of a broken heart; and saveth such as be of a contrite spirit.
>
> Psalm 34:18

Tyndale then includes faith as part of repentance. This comes as no surprise to anyone who has observed the frequency of passages equating faith and repentance together and using them interchangeably. But just how does faith intersect with repentance? Simply put, the sinner who repents of his sin and cries out to God to save him from those sins and their punishment is demonstrating profound and complete trust – or faith – in God to do so. Why else would he call on the name of the Lord in repentance? He who repents trusts in God to forgive and save. One author put it this way:

> "He that believeth," implies repentance. "Repent and be converted," involves faith...Faith is the open hand, relatively to the gift; repentance is the same hand, relatively, not only to the gift but more especially to the dagger that is flung from it...Repentance looks within, faith looks above.[154]

Fourthly, Tyndale noted that, after saving repentance has worked in the sinner, the result is a changed person, a saint who was once a child of wrath but is now a son of God. There is a growing sentiment within fundamentalism that it is routine and normal for Christians to backslide or never demonstrate fruit after being saved. This is not the teaching of the Bible, which makes it clear that repentance changes the soul and makes it a new creature with new desires, beliefs, and actions. True saints, by and large, do not live like the lost. This is where works come in ("fruits meet for repentance"[155]). The repentance in the heart and mind then becomes repentance in deed.

> Therefore if any man be in Christ, he is a new creature: old things are passed away; behold, all things are become new.
>   II Corinthians 5:17

> But, beloved, we are persuaded better things of you, and things that accompany salvation, though we thus speak.
>   Hebrews 6:9

Repentance Is Intent

It is this change of mind regarding actions, committed or intended, that produces a regenerated heart and changed life. True repentance is not a work, but an intention. Some have claimed they felt the burden of conviction fall away the moment they stepped into the aisle to go up front and be saved. They firmly believe salvation occurred before they ever even knelt in prayer. One gospel tract recorded the testimony of Charles McCormick, who wrote:

He who repents trusts in God to forgive and save.

> I decided to go straight to my apartment and pray all night, or pray until God revealed to me that my sins were forgiven. But the very instant I purposed to do this, that heavy burden left.[156]

Critics of repentance from sin simply have no basis for calling this doctrine a works-based gospel. This doctrine simply does not call for works before salvation, and yet the intent to submit to God and all His commands is vital in bringing about the true regeneration that produces righteous and holy Christians. The reason we have dead churches and apostate preachers is because we have a dead gospel and a meaningless salvation. No one is truly born again if they refuse to yield to God's will. Reciting every sin they ever committed is not necessary, but any sin the Holy Ghost convicts them of is that which must be surrendered. Sin as a whole must be surrendered to the Master. Otherwise, there can be no new birth. God resists the proud.

Repentance is a change of mind and heart regarding actions, committed or intended, resulting in a change of course. It is the complete surrender of the rebel to God. Repentance is not the ritual of confession or the bribery of penance. It is not merely sorrow. It is not the sinner mending his ways or trying really hard not to sin. True repentance, as defined and described throughout the Bible, is a sinner agreeing with God about his sins, his inadequacy to save himself, and his need for a Savior. Repentance is the intention to serve God, no matter what. It is the removal of self from the throne of the heart and acknowledging God as supreme, instead.

In summary, consider this eloquent description of the change of heart and mind that is biblical repentance from Paris Reidhead's book, *Finding the Reality of God*:

> Repentance is defined by the Scriptures as a change of mind, turning away from the intention and purpose of pleasing self, and choosing to please God. The seed of all righteousness and holiness is in repentance. Perhaps a man's purpose – his aim and direction – is to please himself. But when he repents he must make an about-face. This is a complete turnabout.
>
> From that moment on, the intention of this man is to please and glorify God – to satisfy only Him. The salvation of which Jesus speaks is not our being satisfied with Him, rather it is His being satisfied with us. Can you see how fatal it is to neglect the salvation that comes in repentance?[157]

Chapter 6

THE GOSPEL TURN

*To open their eyes, and to turn them from darkness to
light, and from the power of Satan unto God, that they
may receive forgiveness of sins, and inheritance among
them which are sanctified by faith that is in me.*
                                                Acts 26:18

This chapter concludes a logical syllogism and will apply
the two principles we have established in the prior two chapters to
the gospel to prove once and for all that gospel repentance is a turn
from sin. In Chapter 4, it was made abundantly plain that repentance,
regardless of how it is defined, is certainly a biblical requirement for
salvation. This is typically agreed upon, even by Antinomians, and
yet there is some controversy surrounding this point, so establishing it
from Scripture was necessary groundwork for the ensuing chapters. In
Chapter 5, the term, *repentance*, was defined biblically. There can no
longer be any doubt that the Bible uses this term almost exclusively to
indicate a turn or change of heart and mind from an action, committed
or intended, resulting in a change of course – and in the context of
humanity, that action is almost always sinful. These are the undeniable
facts as established prior to this chapter. And when viewed together,
they can only lead to one logical conclusion: that a turn from sin is a
gospel requirement.

A syllogism is a very useful rhetorical tool that allows specific
truths to be determined in a given situation using deduction. As long

as the first two statements, or *premises,* in a three-statement syllogism are true, then the third statement, or *conclusion*, must also be true necessarily. For example, consider this simplistic syllogism:

> *Premise 1*: Rover is a dog.
> *Premise 2:* Dogs are mammals.
> *Conclusion:* Ergo, Rover is a mammal.

If it is true that Rover is indeed a dog, and if it is true that dogs are indeed mammals, then it simply cannot be denied that Rover is a mammal. There is no room for doubt or debate, providing the two premises are correct. Chapters 4 and 5 have demonstrated two premises as absolutely true, and now, this chapter will explore the undeniable conclusion that must logically follow from these two premises. To put it plainly, our syllogism reads as follows:

> *Premise 1:* According to the Bible, repentance is required for salvation.
> *Premise 2:* In the context of mankind, repentance means to turn from sin.
> *Conclusion:* Ergo, turning from sin is required for salvation.

If there is any doubt in the mind of the reader regarding the accuracy of either of these two premises, review Chapters 4 and 5 again. But if they are indeed accurate, as I believe we have adequately proven from the Bible, then it is the inescapable, undeniable conclusion that the gospel requires a turn from sin. There can be no other conclusion.

If the premises are true, the conclusion must also be true necessarily.

Thus Saith the Lord

Not only is this the logical conclusion we must reach, it is also borne out in Scripture. Just as there are numerous passages teaching that repentance (regardless of the definition) is required for salvation, and just as there are numerous passages teaching that repentance typically means to turn from sin, there are also numerous passages teaching that the gospel requires turning from sin. This syllogism of Scriptures is condensed in Appendix B. It should be noted that some of these Scriptures do not even use the word, "repent." For example, Paul writes about the Christians in Thessalonica, celebrating their salvation, of which he says, "how ye turned to God from idols to serve the living and true God."[158] Idolatry is a sin, and yet the Bible here says salvation involves turning from it. Antinomians will often grant that repentance from the sin of idolatry can be a requirement for salvation, claiming it is part of turning to belief in the true God. But when pressed, they have to concede repentance from more sins than just this.

Another passage teaches that Christians should be able to move on from such doctrinal basics as the gospel, describing it as follows:

> Therefore leaving the principles of the doctrine of Christ, let
> us go on unto perfection; not laying again the foundation of
> repentance from dead works, and of faith toward God,
> Hebrews 6:1

There is some disagreement over what is meant by the phrase, "dead works." While it may also refer to works done to merit salvation on the part of a sinner ignorant of free grace, it is difficult to escape the adjective, "dead." The Bible tells us the wages of sin is "death."[159] And therefore, "dead works" must primarily refer to those works that kill: sins. This passage is here describing the elementary gospel as repentance from sins. At the very least, the phrase could be understood as encompassing both sins in general and the sin of self-righteousness in particular. Of course, the Antinomian is quick to define it only as the latter, and yet this still leaves him with a problem. Self-righteousness, or trying to buy your way to heaven, is still a sin. And Hebrews 6 tells us repenting from it is part of the elementary doctrine of salvation. And so, now, the list of sins the Antinomian must concede repentance from in order to be saved grows even more. He must now admit that salvation requires repentance from the sins of unbelief, idolatry, and self-righteousness. That makes three sins that must be repented of – how many will it take for the Antinomian to admit the gospel requires turning from sin?

There are numerous passages teaching that the gospel requires turning from sin.

In Acts 3, the Bible does not put a limiting number on how many sins must be repented of for salvation. It merely describes it as turning from "sins" as a whole. Observe what conversion is said to entail, paying special attention to the very last phrase:

> Repent ye therefore, and be converted, that your sins may be blotted out, when the times of refreshing shall come from the presence of the Lord.
> Unto you first God, having raised up his Son Jesus, sent him to bless you, in turning away every one of you from his iniquities.
>
> Acts 3:19, 26

Another passage in Acts is often used to argue that the "baptism of repentance" preached by John the Baptist only entailed believing in God, due to this wording:

> Then said Paul, John verily baptized with the baptism of repentance, saying unto the people, that they should believe on him which should come after him, that is, on Christ Jesus.
>
> Acts 19:4

And yet, Matthew 3 tells us this baptism of repentance included more than just belief. It also included its necessary counterpart – confession of sins:

And saying, Repent ye: for the kingdom of heaven is at
hand.
Then went out to him Jerusalem, and all Judaea, and all the
region round about Jordan,
And were baptized of him in Jordan, confessing their sins.

Matthew 3:2, 5-6

Once again, in the book of James, conversion is described as
turning someone from their sins – not just the penalty of sins, but from
the sins, themselves:

Let him know, that he which converteth the sinner from the
error of his way shall save a soul from death, and shall hide
a multitude of sins.

James 5:20

In II Corinthians, Paul the apostle writes about the difference
between temporal or worldly sorrow and permanent or godly sorrow
over sin. While some are quick to do away with this reference,
because the context is a sinful church and not lost people, the simple
fact of the matter is Paul is using this opportunity to lecture on these
two kinds of sorrow and comments on salvation in the process. Surely
no one would pretend a gospel message preached in a church had
nothing to do with lost people or eternal salvation just because it was
spoken to a congregation of generally saved people. So why should
we assume Paul was not speaking of eternal salvation in this passage
simply because his audience is supposedly saved? In this passage,
Paul tells these saved church members that the kind of godly sorrow
they exemplified over specific sins that had come to light in the church
is the same kind of penitent sorrow that leads sinners to be saved:

Now I rejoice, not that ye were made sorry, but that ye
sorrowed to repentance: for ye were made sorry after a godly
manner, that ye might receive damage by us in nothing.

> For godly sorrow worketh repentance to salvation not to be
> repented of: but the sorrow of the world worketh death.
>
> II Corinthians 7:9-10

And so Paul here demonstrates yet again that salvation requires a turn from sin in godly sorrow or repentance. This is one of many New Testament passages we have reviewed thus far that illustrate this logical conclusion. Yet there is an even more clear passage in the Old Testament that tells so much about the gospel of repentance from sin. Read this text carefully, and then we shall examine it piece by piece:

> Seek ye the Lord while he may be found, call ye upon him
> while he is near:
> Let the wicked forsake his way, and the unrighteous man his
> thoughts: and let him return unto the Lord, and he will have
> mercy upon him; and to our God, for he will abundantly
> pardon.
>
> Isaiah 55:6-7

This Old Testament passage, though written before the birth, death, burial, and resurrection of Jesus Christ, provides a complete gospel message for its time. Though it was written before the profound writings of Paul expounded on the gospel message once hidden to those who stumbled at it, here is the essence of the gospel in full display. The passage is replete with meaning, so we will examine each phrase closely:

"Seek ye the Lord while he may be found, call ye upon him while he is near..." – This is a gospel call, echoing the gospel promise reiterated in the New Testament that "whosoever shall call upon the name of the Lord shall be saved."[160]

"Let the wicked...and the unrighteous man..." – This is no call for saints to cease from backsliding, but rather a call to lost people to be born again. It cannot be referring to saints, because the Bible calls saints "righteous"[161] and lost people "unrighteous."[162]

"...forsake his way, and the unrighteous man his thoughts..." – And so, this gospel message calls for a change of thoughts, i.e. a mental turn.

"...and let him return unto the Lord..." – Notice the "turn" in "return." This is doing an about-face and changing direction. This is a change of heart and mind regarding actions, intended or committed, resulting in a change of course. And lest some mistakenly think that "return" indicates these people are saints being called to turn from their backsliding, it is worth pointing out that everyone begins life in a state of innocence, ignorant of the law.[163] Therefore, it is perfectly accurate to tell someone who has never been born again to "return" to God.

"...and he will have mercy upon him..." – Yet again the Bible calls that which God gives those who repent, "mercy." If repentance from sin were works, that which God gave to those who repented would have to be called *wages*, not "mercy."

"...and to our God, for he will abundantly pardon." – Once again, this passage uses terms that show us this is speaking of salvation for sinners, not sanctification for the believer. Saints do not need a pardon, but only forgiveness and restoration of their fellowship with God. But sinners, who stand condemned in God's courtroom,[164] are in need of a full pardon.

> *If repentance from sin were works, that which God gave to those who repented would have to be called wages, not "mercy."*

True Belief vs. False Belief

The Bible tells us even the devils believe in God, and they tremble.[165] In fact, they even acknowledged Jesus as the "Son of

God."[166] What good did it do them? Why are there so many people who claim to have believed in Jesus who either never live for God or only start to before falling back to the world? They said the prayer. They believed in Jesus. What happened? Ask this question of an Antinomian, and he will likely respond that the false convert simply did not truly believe. In fact, there are many Antinomians who reject the simplistic sinner's-prayer approach and the basic *easy-believism* method. While redefining gospel repentance as merely turning from unbelief, they at least do not hold with sales-pitch gospel presentations and high-pressure methods of evangelism. To them, it is not about the prayer, but about the heart. And they are to be applauded for this. But it is not enough.

Their converts typically never come to church, or if they do, they never leave the pew to actually bear fruit in the world. Many of them fall away within a few months or years. Why? Once again, the Antinomian would say because they did not truly believe with all of their heart. He may even quote Philip, who told the Ethiopian Eunuch, "If thou believest with all thine heart,"[167] to emphasize the importance of true belief vs. false belief. But this begs the question: just what is the difference between these two beliefs? What constitutes true belief? What is missing in false belief?

It is my contention that, put simply, the difference between these two beliefs is repentance – the inward turning away from sin. Merely believing in Jesus as the Savior from hell must also be accompanied by the yielding to Him as the Lord and Savior from sin. False belief is that faith which James says is dead, being without works.[168] Works come from a change in intent, also known as repentance. Therefore, the difference between false belief and true belief must lie in the presence or absence of repentance from sin.

There is a general trend to be observed that those who get saved from hell with little to no thought of addressing sin typically do not consider sin a significant problem in the Christian life. And many of them fall away. But conversely, those who are born again and saved from sin through repentance often emphasize holiness in the Christian life and remain faithful to the end. Even those who do not consciously confess their sin when they are converted are often truly born again by the simple and child-like surrender of themselves as a whole to the Master. This is why the Bible does speak of salvation as a simple thing that even a child can grasp. It is not necessary for the convert to have compiled a list of all known sins in his life and surrendered them over, one by one, in a dramatic prayer. And yet this surrender holds nothing back. As the psalmist noted, "If I regard iniquity in my heart, the Lord will not hear me."[169]

Consider the short prayer of the thief on the cross. He acknowledged that he and his fellow malefactor were guilty and deserving of their punishment and humbly asked Jesus to remember him in His kingdom. But that simple, child-like prayer was rich in meaning. Through it, that thief acknowledged himself as the sinner God saw him as, surrendered his rights and will over to God, and humbly asked for mercy, recognizing Jesus as God and Master. This is the essence of repentance, and it is not in a checklist or formula. It is a matter of the heart. True belief contains repentance, surrender, and a new perspective.

The great author, Harry Ironside, wrote on this difference between mere intellectual belief and a change of heart and mind regarding sin and God. He even credits the Antinomians as the source for the modern heresy that divides saving faith from repentance:

> ...the faith that justifies is not a mere intellectual process – not merely crediting certain historical facts or doctrinal statements; but it is a faith that springs from a divinely wrought conviction of sin which produces a repentance that is sincere and genuine...Repentance is not opposed to grace; it is the recognition of the need of grace...Yet there are not wanting professed preachers of grace who, like the Antinomians of old, decry the necessity of repentance lest it seem to invalidate the freedom of grace.[170]

True Belief Is Directional

While the Antinomian scratches his head at the puzzle of how so many who believe on Christ can be false converts, and at how unperceivable the difference is between true and false belief, the missing piece of this puzzle is to be found in repentance from sin. False belief is vain and empty. It does not require anything of the sinner. Yes, true faith requires something, though it is not meritorious in the least. And that which it requires is to run to the Savior. If a church offers free meals to any homeless person who comes to their kitchen, this does not require a work. The homeless person does not earn his meal by walking through the door. Likewise, free grace is given to those with faith that causes them to run to the Savior, leaving behind their sins, affections, self-righteousness, idols, and rebellion.

> *True belief contains repentance, surrender, and a new perspective.*

In his landmark parable of the Christian life, *Pilgrim's Progress,* John Bunyan records a powerful monologue from a Christian named Hopeful. Hopeful is explaining how he came to be born again, and he describes the point in his search when he asked God how to believe. Though he felt within him the need to trust in the Lord Jesus Christ, he found himself unsure and inept. He discovered that true belief is the kind that causes the sinner to run after the Savior with all of his heart, soul, and might:

> But, Lord, what is believing? And then I saw from that saying – "He that cometh to me shall never hunger, and he that believeth on me shall never thirst" – that believing and coming was all one; and that he that came, that is, ran out in his heart and his affections after salvation by Christ, he indeed believed in Christ.[171]

Believing and coming – or turning to Christ – are all one. The sinner who repents, truly believes. And the sinner who truly believes, repents. This is the essence of true faith. False belief changes no one and requires no real change of direction. But true belief requires a complete change of perspective, loyalty, and desires. This is why Jesus likened the kingdom of heaven to a pearl of great price. The Bible says the merchant man who found this pearl "sold all that he had"[172] in order to acquire it. Nothing he owned was too precious to give up for it.

This is reminiscent of another account in the Bible in which the kingdom of heaven was so precious that Jesus expected a rich, young ruler to sell all that he had to gain it. But the young man went away offended. If belief was so cheap that it did not require anything of the young man, why then did Jesus not run after him and tell him to forget about selling all he owned? After all, according to Antinomianism, that would be adding works to the gospel, anyway. "Just believe in me," He could have said. But He didn't. He told him to take up his cross and follow Him, to effectively die to self and selfish desires. He let that young man walk away and go to hell, stifled by his unwillingness to make the transaction because the price was too high.

And this is the difference between false belief and true belief. False belief costs nothing. True belief costs everything. It costs our will, our affections, our allegiance, and all of our sins. Inherent in the call to take up the cross is the call to forsake everything in repentance. Does God expect us to make an itemized list and give each item up in prayer? Of course not. But nothing can be held back. If the love of money and greed are your sins, those will be the sins God expects you to give up before you can ask for mercy. "If I regard iniquity in my heart, the Lord will not hear me," the Bible says.[173]

During the siege of Israel in the days of Elisha, there were four lepers sitting at the gate of Samaria.[174] Rather than sit there until destruction came upon them, they decided to go outside the city to the camp of the Syrians to see if their fate could improve. The way

False belief costs nothing. True belief costs everything. It costs our will, our affections, our allegiance, and all of our sins.

they saw things, death awaited them either from their leprosy or from the Syrian attack that would soon come. Things could get no worse. And so they decided to leave and see if they might improve their lot by surrendering to their enemy, the Syrians. Perhaps they could at least receive a meal or two. But when they arrived at the Syrian camp, they found that God had chased away the host in such a hurry that they had left all their food and treasure in the camp. The lepers were suddenly very wealthy and very well-fed men.

Sinners today are faced with a very similar circumstance. They are diseased with the leprosy of sin and await imminent destruction. But rather than see themselves this way, most sinners consider themselves to be good people. They have no need to run out and surrender to the enemy; they like their lot in life fine enough. But repentance changes this. True belief leads them to see their situation in a completely different light. No longer are they wealthy, but paupers. No longer are they healthy, but diseased. No longer are they fed, but starving. And Jesus says, "He that cometh to me shall never hunger."[175] True belief causes them to turn and run into the other camp. Leaving behind everything they own, sinners who truly trust in the promises of Christ run out in their hearts and affections to Christ in complete repentance and surrender, no matter what the result will be. And when they arrive at the feet of the cross, clinging to nothing of their own, they find mercy. This is the gospel turn.

This complete, directional change can be found in the prayer of Job after he was rebuked by Elihu and God. He saw himself as completely filthy compared to God's holiness and decided to stop going down the path he was on:

Behold, I am vile; what shall I answer thee? I will lay mine
hand upon my mouth.
Once have I spoken; but I will not answer: yea, twice; but I
will proceed no further.

Job 40:4-5

Job saw himself in the light of God's glory and put his hand
to his mouth. No more excuses. He proceeded no more, because he
was changing direction. Though Job was already a child of God and
did not become born again in this particular passage, his prayer is
nonetheless a vivid illustration of the kind of turn required of the lost.
And that turn is a gift of God called repentance. As noted biblical
scholar and missionary, David Cloud, stated:

> Repentance is a supernatural work of God whereby a
> responsive sinner, being convicted by the Holy Spirit of his
> rebellion, turns to God from his sinful ways and trusts Jesus
> Christ for salvation.[176]

A Turn of Heart and Mind

We have seen how the Bible requires a turn from sin to the
Savior in order to be saved. Yet it must be underscored that this turn
begins in the mind and heart and is therefore not a meritorious work.
Salvation is a free gift that cannot be earned. But neither can it be
given to someone actively fleeing from God. Repentance is granted to
the sinner in the mind and heart before it ever manifests in the godly
actions of a true believer. In Webster's 1828 dictionary, one definition
for *turn* is, "To change the mind or conduct."[177] And so the cause and
effect are so intimately connected that they can both be referred to as
repentance, but it is this change of mind and heart that God looks at
when reconciling a sinner to Himself. And thus God says that, when
sinners come to repentance – or the gospel turn – He will give them
"mercy."[178]

The Bible not only tells us clearly that repentance is necessary
for salvation, it also defines the term for us. And then, as though that

were not enough, the Word of God also provides us with passages that plainly explain a turn from sin to the Savior is required for salvation. A white flag of surrender must be waived. Attitudes and intentions must be changed. And the treasonous sinner must run out to God in true faith and repentance, leaving all behind.

Depth of Mercy
I have long withstood His grace,
Long provoked Him to His face,
Would not hearken to His calls,
Grieved Him by a thousand falls.
Now incline me to repent,
Let me now my sins lament;
Now my foul revolt deplore,
Weep, believe, and sin no more.
Charles Wesley[179]

Chapter 7
SAVED FROM SIN

And she shall bring forth a son, and thou shalt call his name Jesus: for he shall save his people from their sins.

Matthew 1:21

The ancient Antinomians did not consider the law to be of use in the Christian life or the gospel, nor did they thus consider transgressing that law – sin – to be of significance to either. Likewise, modern Antinomians have little regard for God's law and thus do not view salvation through God's eyes, but through man's. To the modern Antinomian, the gospel saves unbelievers from unbelief so they can go to heaven. But to God, the gospel saves sinners from their sin and pays their sin debt so they can be conformed to His image. Having established that the gospel requires repentance from sin, let us now turn our attention to the question of why. What is the purpose of the gospel, and why is repentance from sin such an integral part of it?

Why Are Sinners Damned?

The first issue that must be addressed is just what it is that sends a person to hell. Why are sinners damned? Is it unbelief that damns them or sin? To the Antinomian, the idea that sin would be so significant as to send someone to hell is utterly repugnant. After all, God is a loving and forgiving God, and sin is just "missing the mark."[180]

How could a little thing like sin be the cause for God to send someone to hell? Jack Hyles, the pastor of First Baptist of Hammond, Indiana, and renowned for his gross immorality, propelled Antinomianism to prominence among fundamentalists in the late 20th century. He came out solidly in favor of the view that it is only unbelief that damns the sinner. To Hyles – as well as to the many thousands of minds he influenced – the only reason someone goes to hell was because they did not believe on Christ. Therefore, the only sin that must be repented of to be saved is unbelief. In other words, the moment a lost soul turns away from unbelief and to belief, they are saved. Hyles had this to say in his widely circulated *Enemies of Soul Winning*:

> A person who does not believe is condemned, so not believing is what makes a person lost…we have to repent only of the thing that makes us unsaved, and that is unbelief.[181]

It is certainly logical to conclude that one must repent of that which makes one lost, but it is the height of logical absurdity to conclude that the thing that makes one lost is not believing in that which saves. This is circular. The situation can be illustrated by the metaphor of a snakebite victim. If someone is bitten by a very venomous snake and dies, the coroner would no doubt conclude that the person had died from the venom of the snake. But if that snakebite victim was given the opportunity to receive an antivenom to counteract the venom, and refused it, the cause of death would still be the snake's venom. In such a case, the coroner would never conclude that the cause of death was refusal to accept the antivenom. Anyone reading such a report would ask what had happened to the victim to require him to need the antivenom in the first place. Though the victim most likely would have survived if he had accepted the medicine, it was not the lack of that antivenom medicine that killed him. It was still the venom. Likewise, the sinner will be saved if he repents in true faith, yet it is not his lack of faith that starts him on the path to hell. Damnation is not the result of unbelief, though trusting in Christ would certainly counter it. Damnation is the result of sin. This is not only logical but the clear teaching of Scripture. Consider Paul's accounting of the origin of death in his epistle to the Romans:

> Wherefore, as by one man sin entered into the world, and death by sin; and so death passed upon all men, for that all have sinned:[182]

Sin brought death into the world. Before Adam's sin, man was to live forever. But sin changed everything. It doomed him to physical death, but also to eternal death in what the Bible calls the "second death"[183] in the Lake of Fire. Indeed, in the very next chapter, Paul contrasts eternal life with the death brought about by sin, making the point that sin results in eternal death:

Damnation is not the result of unbelief, though trusting in Christ would certainly counter it. Damnation is the result of sin.

> For the wages of sin is death; but the gift of God is eternal life through Jesus Christ our Lord.[184]

But Paul uses even stronger language elsewhere in the New Testament, so there will be no doubt as to why a loving and merciful God eternally damns souls to hell. And he by no means lays the blame entirely at the feet of unbelief. In fact, he even provides a list of sins that bring about the eternal wrath of God upon the sinner:

> Mortify therefore your members which are upon the earth; fornication, uncleanness, inordinate affection, evil concupiscence, and covetousness, which is idolatry:
> For which things' sake the wrath of God cometh on the children of disobedience:
>
> Colossians 3:5-6

And just in case the reader does not believe this an emphatic enough statement as to the cause of God's wrath falling on the sinner, Paul states elsewhere the same thing in even stronger terms:

> For this ye know, that no whoremonger, nor unclean person, nor covetous man, who is an idolater, hath any inheritance in the kingdom of Christ and of God.
> Let no man deceive you with vain words: for because of these things cometh the wrath of God upon the children of disobedience.
>
> Ephesians 5:5-6

Notice Paul's warning about letting others deceive with vain words. Surely the words of false prophets like Jack Hyles fit this description. His words contradict God's almost diametrically. In his attack on biblical repentance, Hyles commented on John 3:36, which states that "the wrath of God abideth" on "he that believeth not the Son." Rather than acknowledge the verse never contradicts the writings of Paul in Romans, Ephesians, or Colossians, and never says this sinner originally came under wrath because of this unbelief, Hyles directly contradicts God's words, stating:

> What makes the wrath of God abide on a person? Believing not! So, from what must a person repent in order to be saved? He must repent of that which makes him lost.[185]

Condemned Already

Preachers like Jack Hyles and former Hyles-Anderson student, Pastor Steven Anderson, make much ado about John 3:18, as though it proves that only unbelief damns the sinner, when really the verse says something entirely different:

> He that believeth on him is not condemned: but he that believeth not is condemned already, because he hath not believed in the name of the only begotten Son of God.
>
> John 3:18

While it is true that this verse states that those who believe will not be condemned, it never says condemnation comes *from* unbelief. Yet this is precisely what the antinomian crowd teaches out of this verse, as though the mere presence of the words, "believeth not" and "believed," prove an either-or situation: either you believe and don't get condemned or you don't believe and are punished with condemnation for it. But just look at the passage again. The answer is right there. What is this passage actually saying? One little word clears up the entire matter instantly: "already." The sinner is not condemned because of mere unbelief. The unbeliever is under condemnation "already," because of his *sins*! The only reason he is in need of a Savior in whom to believe is because of the sin that has "already" brought him under condemnation. This is demonstrated plainly in the very next verse, which tells us the condemnation came because of the sinner's love for darkness and evil deeds – not because of their unbelief:

> And this is the condemnation, that light is come into the world, and men loved darkness rather than light, because their deeds were evil.
>
> John 3:19

Unbelief on the part of the sinner is simply the rejection of the medicine he desperately needs because he suffers from the bite of the serpent. With the venom of sin coursing through the sinner's veins, he is in need of the antidote which comes through repentance toward God and faith toward our Lord Jesus Christ.[186] Without that antidote, he will die eternally in the Lake of Fire – not from lack of the antidote, but from the poison of sin inside him!

Unfortunately, the antinomian gospel fails to warn sinners they are already infected with the disease of sin. Rather than give them eternal victory over that sin today, the antinomian gospel promises healing only from a future disease that the sinner does not yet have – hell. In shifting the focus away from sin and to eternal bliss in heaven, Antinomians ignore that sinners are already under God's condemnation and estranged from Him. They ignore the need for sinners to be reconciled to their God. They ignore the present cure for a present disease. In its place, the Antinomians promise a future solution for a future, somewhat theoretical, illness – hell. And so their converts live in sin, completely undelivered from its power in the present, because they were only saved from a future hell. Getting saved from a future ill will never produce a present benefit.

This is not to diminish the seriousness of hellfire which will befall those who do not repent of their sins. The verdict of Scripture is plain: God will cast sinners into the Lake of Fire because of their works, not just their unbelief:

> And I saw the dead, small and great, stand before God; and the books were opened: and another book was opened, which is the book of life: and the dead were judged out of those things which were written in the books, according to their works.
> And the sea gave up the dead which were in it; and death and hell delivered up the dead which were in them: and they were judged every man according to their works.
>
> Revelation 20:12-13

The sinner is not condemned because of mere unbelief... The only reason he is in need of a Savior in whom to believe is because of the sin that has 'already' brought him under condemnation.

For some, this passage must present a real problem, because it appears to teach works-salvation. After all, if we are saved by grace through faith, what do our works have to do with the final determination? But the Bible plainly teaches that only those who have been born again will be allowed to forgo this examination. Works do not enter the picture for saints who have partaken of the new birth. But those who have not believed will be judged according to their works. They will be cast into the Lake of Fire based on one criterion: their sin. The Antinomians will often claim it is improper to preach the law to sinners, since God only holds saints responsible for their actions, yet the Bible declares they "shall be judged by the law."[187]

Antinomians like Steven Anderson, who founded the *Repentance Blacklist* website and rails against repentance from sin, will point to John 16:9 to prove that repentance has only to do with unbelief. But once again, if we pay close attention, it will become clear that this passage actually supports our premise that sin is what damns the sinner, and not merely unbelief:

> And when he is come, he will reprove the world of sin, and
> of righteousness, and of judgment:
> Of sin, because they believe not on me.
>
> John 16:8-9

Anderson dismisses this passage with little effort to actually address what it says. After yelling the line, "because they believe not on me!" for emphasis when reading this text, he then gives this baseless and empty explanation, smacking of Antinomianism:

> So what is the reproving the world of sin about? Because they believe not on Him...What does that have to do with turning over a new leaf anywhere in that passage? What does that have to do with a guilty feeling? Nothing. Nothing. It's turning from not believing to believing. It's turning from a false doctrine to the true doctrine of Jesus Christ.[188]

This passage does not teach that sin is insignificant and that the only thing that matters in the gospel is having the right doctrine. This passage does not teach that sinners are damned only because of unbelief. Quite the contrary! This passage tells us explicitly that they are damned for "sin," and then it tells us exactly why their sins are at issue: because they believed not on Christ. As Revelation 20 demonstrated, sinners must be judged according to their sins since they did not believe, whereas saints are judged according to Christ's blood since they did believe. If sinners will trust in Christ with genuine repentance and faith, they will not be judged according to their works. But because they do not, then they are damned for their sins, as is repeated in Revelation:

Sinners must be judged according to their sins, whereas saints are judged according to Christ's blood.

> But the fearful, and unbelieving, and the abominable, and murderers, and whoremongers, and sorcerers, and idolaters, and all liars, shall have their part in the lake which burneth with fire and brimstone: which is the second death.
>
> Revelation 21:8

Here the Bible once again provides a list of sins that will bring about damnation, and unbelief is only one in a list. Make no mistake; unbelief is a sin. Unbelief means doubting the words of God, not following His commands, and rejecting His provision. Sinners will pay for this sin in hell. But this is only one of the many sins they will pay for when they are judged according to their works rather than the blood of Jesus. If they had only believed, their works would never enter the picture. But because they did not believe, they will be judged based on their sins.

Questions Raised

If sinners are damned only for unbelief, and not for their sins, then God has a lot of explaining to do. There are many questions that remain unanswered in the Bible if the antinomian gospel is correct. For example, Romans 2 declares that even those heathen who have never heard of Christ will be judged and sent to hell. Why? How can God possibly be just and fair in sending to hell those who never even had the chance to reject Him? The answer is quite simply that they are not judged for their unbelief in, or rejection of, a Savior they never even heard of. They are judged for their sin like everyone else. You see, God does not owe mankind a Savior. And it is quite possible that some heathen have died in their sins having never heard the gospel or even of the Savior. But God is still holy and just and fair to damn them because they lived and died in rebellion against God (a God every man is born with the knowledge of[189]). It is for their sin they deserve hell and not for rejecting the gospel of Jesus Christ. Indeed, Paul tells us in Romans 2 that it has nothing to do with whether or not they heard, but whether or not they obeyed the law of God written on the heart of every man, woman, and child:

> (For not the hearers of the law are just before God, but the doers of the law shall be justified.
> For when the Gentiles, which have not the law, do by nature the things contained in the law, these, having not the law, are a law unto themselves:
> Which shew the work of the law written in their hearts, their conscience also bearing witness, and their thoughts the mean while accusing or else excusing one another;)
> Romans 2:13-15

But this is not the only question raised by the antinomian view. If sinners are damned only because of unbelief, why did Jesus point out the sins of sinners, from the woman at the well to the rich, young ruler? If their sin was not the problem, why not limit the message to belief or unbelief? In fact, why does the Bible tell us the law is useful in drawing the sinner to God?

> Wherefore the law was our schoolmaster to bring us unto
> Christ, that we might be justified by faith.
>
> Galatians 3:24

If sin were not the issue God had with the lost, the question must be asked, why is the law to be their schoolmaster? What does the law teach about belief? Obviously, the answer is that justification by faith comes because the guilt of sin is pointed out by the standard of God's law. Sinners who do not obey God's law are to be brought to the point of godly sorrow for their sin, at which point they are often led to run to the Savior, so they will not have to be judged by their works. If salvation does not require repentance from sin, neither does it require the law as a schoolmaster.

In Mark 9:43-48, Jesus warns sinners to go so far in avoiding sin as to cut off their own hands and pluck out their own eyes to avoid hellfire. But if sin is not what damns the sinner to hell, then this raises yet another question: how could their members send them to hell? Why would the Savior warn sinners to amputate their own members to avoid sin if unbelief was all they should be concerned with? How could their members keep them from saving faith? These questions can only be answered by one conclusion. The Bible means what it says when it warns sinners to flee from sin and to the Savior. Physical members are often the instruments by which sinners commit sins and thus earn damnation in hell. The Bible declares sin is the disease that damns sinners to hell, not merely unbelief, and repentance from that sin is what constitutes saving faith and deliverance.

What Are You Saved From?

Leonard Ravenhill was a noted author and evangelist in the 20th century and often focused on themes of holiness and revival. In his sermons and books, he bemoaned the cheap, meaningless brand of so-called salvation most pew warmers professed. He once asked his audience:

> Are you saved? What are you saved from, hell? Are you saved from bitterness? Are you saved from lust? Are you saved from cheating? Are you saved from lying? Are you saved from bad manners? Are you saved from rebellion against your parents? Come on, what are you saved from?[190]

Today's antinomian Christian has no victory over present sin. He lives a powerless and sinful life. He tells himself that everyone sins, and that is just how it will be until Jesus comes back – but no big deal, because his sins are paid for. But this is an insult to the very purpose for which Christ died! Jesus did not leave His throne, put on a robe of flesh, dwell among us, and then die at the hands of His own creation just so we could go to heaven. Christ died to save souls from not only the penalty of past sin,

Why would the Savior warn sinners to amputate their own members to avoid sin if unbelief was all they should be concerned with?

but also from the power of present sin. The believer who truly has been made a new creature is empowered with the supernatural ability to resist the devil, flee youthful lusts, and oppose the wickedness of the world in which he lives. This is why the Bible describes God's saints as pure and blameless – not only because of their eternally redeemed standing before God, but also because of their ongoing state of sanctification and holiness. Are Christians utterly sinless? Of course not. They still have the sinful body of flesh vying for control. But sin should be such an exceptionally rare event in the life of the believer, that when he does stumble and fall, it grieves him and is utterly intolerable in his life. Contrast this with the Antinomian, who is perfectly at home in a sinful state, here a little sin, there a little sin. To the Antinomian, Psalm 24 should be rewritten to say:

> Who shall ascend into the hill of the Lord? or who shall stand in his holy place?
> He that hath semi-clean hands, and a less-than-pure heart; who hath not lifted up his soul unto vanity most of the time, nor sworn deceitfully, except when needed.
> He shall receive the blessing from the Lord, and a get-out-of-hell-free card from the God of his salvation.
> This is the generation of them that seek him on Sunday mornings, that seek thy face sometimes, O Jacob. Selah.

What a mockery carnal Antinomianism makes of the consecrated life of the saint! It cheapens the power of the blood of Jesus and diminishes the very purpose of the gospel, which, in addition to satisfying God's wrath, was also to conform us to God's image and defeat the power of sin. This is what we should learn from the gospel. This is what saving grace teaches the believer according to the words of Paul to Titus:

> For the grace of God that bringeth salvation hath appeared to all men,
> Teaching us that, denying ungodliness and worldly lusts, we should live soberly, righteously, and godly, in this present world;
> Looking for that blessed hope, and the glorious appearing of the great God and our Saviour Jesus Christ;
> Who gave himself for us, that he might redeem us from all iniquity, and purify unto himself a peculiar people, zealous of good works.
>
> Titus 2:11-14

Not only does this passage confirm that the purpose of the gospel was to "redeem us from all iniquity" – and not just from hell or the single sin of unbelief – but also that the gospel teaches holiness. Why? Because we are crucified with Christ[191] and therefore dead

indeed unto sin.[192]   Our flesh and its power over us are crucified by
the gospel, and we are alive unto righteousness. This is the message
of the gospel. But the antinomian gospel ignores or diminishes this.
The great 19th-century commentator, Matthew Henry, observed in the
repentance gospel of John the Baptist that the gospel which included
repentance from sin would teach men to be holy, and that this was its
very design:

> He bound them, not to such ceremonious observances as
> were imposed by the tradition of the elders, but to change
> their mind, and change their way, to cast away from them all
> their transgressions, and to make them new hearts and to live
> new lives. The design of the gospel, which now began, was
> to make men devout and pious, holy and heavenly, humble
> and meek, sober and chaste, just and honest, charitable
> and kind, and good in every relation, who had been much
> otherwise; and this is to repent.[193]

In his comments on Isaiah 45, Henry – who by no means could
be said to have taught works salvation – went even further, arguing
that salvation essentially *is* righteousness, and the two are inseparable.
Regeneration is God making men righteous, and the two simply cannot
be divided:

> We must not expect salvation without righteousness, for
> they spring up together and together the Lord hath created
> them; what he has joined together, let not us therefore put
> asunder. See Ps. 85:9-11. Christ died to save us from our
> sins, not in our sins, and is made redemption to us by being
> made to us righteousness and sanctification.[194]

Indeed, the Bible at times uses the terms interchangeably. In
the language of the Bible, God views salvation as righteousness. For
example, consider Romans 10:9-10, that often-memorized passage on
the gospel. It is seldom noticed that, in verse nine, regeneration is

referred to as, "be saved," but in the next verse, it is referred to as both "salvation" and "righteousness:"

> That if thou shalt confess with thy mouth the Lord Jesus, and shalt believe in thine heart that God hath raised him from the dead, thou shalt be saved.
> For with the heart man believeth unto righteousness; and with the mouth confession is made unto salvation.
> Romans 10:9-10

Pay close attention to the following passages. While it is the common view that the gospel primarily saves from hell (humanism), the true primary design of the gospel is stated in many places in Scripture:

> And she shall bring forth a son, and thou shalt call his name Jesus: for he shall save his people from their sins.
> Matthew 1:21

> To open their eyes, and to turn them from darkness to light, and from the power of Satan unto God, that they may receive forgiveness of sins, and inheritance among them which are sanctified by faith that is in me.
> Acts 26:18

> But he that lacketh these things is blind, and cannot see afar off, and hath forgotten that he was purged from his old sins.
> II Peter 1:9

"Christ died to save us from our sins, not in our sins, and is made redemption to us by being made to us righteousness and sanctification."

Because the Antinomian disregards the law of God and the holiness of God, he likewise does not understand the gospel as a way to overcome sin. To him, the secondary purpose of the gospel – saving souls from eternal damnation – is the only or the primary purpose. Harry Ironside once observed that "Low thoughts of sin come from low thoughts of God's holiness and righteousness."[195] Those who encounter the holiness of God when they are redeemed will never be satisfied until they, too, are holy and sanctified. And they will properly understand their place in God's economy, resulting in a more balanced understanding of the gospel and righteousness.

"Low thoughts of sin come from low thoughts of God's holiness and righteousness."

Conformed to His Image

Because God is holy, He cannot fellowship with those who are not. In fact, He cannot even look upon sin.[196] The Bible insists that sin – mutiny against God's authority – puts up a wall of separation between the sinner and God:

> Behold, the Lord's hand is not shortened, that it cannot save; neither his ear heavy, that it cannot hear:
> But your iniquities have separated between you and your God, and your sins have hid his face from you, that he will not hear.
>
> Isaiah 59:1-2

Until the penalty for the sin is paid and the sinner becomes a new creature, God cannot look upon the face of the lost person. He cannot hear their prayer or commune with them. Their sin is too offensive and must be put way. This is the justice of God. The great evangelist, George Whitefield, recorded in his journal praying, "Give us such a sense of Thy justice as to convince us that we cannot be saved if we continue in sin."[197] Whitefield understood that God does not accept the sinner still actively engaged in his sins. Those sins must be put away and blotted out of God's sight. Fortunately, God is also merciful and provided a way for those sins to be put away and

the sinner to be conformed to an image pleasing to the Lord – but
that mercy requires repentance from sin because turning merely from
unbelief does not address that which is offensive to God:

> Repent ye therefore, and be converted, that your sins may
> be blotted out, when the times of refreshing shall come from
> the presence of the Lord.
>
> Acts 3:19

It is interesting to note that these words were spoken after the
cross, and yet Peter tells these sinners they still need their sins blotted
out. There is a strain of Antinomian thought that concludes all sin was
blotted out by the cross, and therefore all sin committed after Calvary
is taken care of. All that remains is to turn from unbelief. And yet
here, after the cross, sin is said to be still on the books for unrepentant
sinners. And it has contorted them into wretches too disfigured for
God to look upon, in need of His refreshing and conversion.

This view of the sinner as ugly and offensive before God
goes against the grain of the Antinomian. It does not sit well within
his unbiblical philosophy tainted with humanism. And yet this is
precisely how God sees the sinner – a wicked, undeserving wretch
and a monster of iniquity. And it is for this reason that God allowed
for the gospel to change men, to make them holy and suitable for His
fellowship. Because mankind was utterly incapable of ever reaching
this level on his own, God provided the gospel as a means to conform
treasonous monsters into sanctified saints. Paul asserts in Romans
that "whom he did foreknow, he also did predestinate to be conformed
to the image of his Son."[198] Though that process will not be complete
until glorification at Christ's return, the conversion occurs at salvation
and is intended to completely transform the sinner and put him on the
path to looking more and more like Christ. The Bible says:

> Therefore if any man be in Christ, he is a new creature: old
> things are passed away; behold, all things are become new.
>
> II Corinthians 5:17

The Antinomian overlooks this beautiful promise of God regarding the work of regeneration. To the Antinomian who does not view sin as heinous or salvation as the remedy for a sinful disfigurement, this passage must mean very little. To him, the gospel is merely a promise of future benefits, not a transformation from death unto life and from the ugliness of iniquity unto the beauty of holiness.[199] Observe this point powerfully articulated in the favorite holiday hymn, "Hark! the Herald Angels Sing," which puts this very doctrine to music:

> Rise, the woman's conq'ring seed,
> Bruise in us the serpent's head.
> Adam's likeness now efface,
> Stamp thine image in its place:
> Second Adam from above,
> Reinstate us in Thy love.[200]

In Adam, our race was marred with sin, separated from God, and cursed for generations. But in the Second Adam, Christ redeemed our race from the dreadful effects of sin's curse. He put away the sin that separated us from our Creator, thus reinstating us in His fellowship. Because of the gospel, those who once bore the resemblance of their father, the devil, can be given a new family resemblance. Because of the gospel, we are no longer bound to do the works of the devil, but can now be free from the power of sin. In repentance, the sinner is given righteousness, by which it is evident that he is a new creature. George Whitefield wrote briefly in his journal of an encounter with an Antinomian and commented on the changing power of the gospel in the life of the sinner, who, having renounced sin, may now live in that righteousness which identifies a believer as such:

> Had a conference after sermon with one, who I fear with some others, maintained antinomian principles. From such, may all that know them turn away; for though, (to use the words of our Church Article) good works, which are the fruits of faith, cannot put away our sins, or endure the

severity of God's judgment (that is, cannot justify us), yet
they follow after justification, and do spring out necessarily
of a true and lively faith, insomuch that by them a lively
faith may be as evidently known as a tree discerned by the
fruit.[201]

A Change of Lordship

Lordship Salvation is a term used derogatorily to refer to those
who teach repentance from sin in the gospel. While some may go
too far with this doctrine and stray into works salvation, generally,
those who are labeled with this term merely point out that salvation
changes the allegiance of the sinner and frees them from the power of
sin to serve the living Christ. We have already established that this
is precisely what the gospel accomplishes and the purpose for which
it was designed by God. In the Old Testament, Micah prophesied of
this Redeemer using the military term, "subdue," in reference to sin:

> He will turn again, he will have compassion upon us; he will
> subdue our iniquities; and thou wilt cast all their sins into
> the depths of the sea.
> > Micah 7:19

The reason we see such strong wording is simply because God
sees the sin problem as the ultimate problem resolved by the gospel.
Mankind has been at war with God since the fall of Adam, and the
gospel is the chosen mechanism to end the war on an individual level
and restore the son of Adam to God. This could not be stated more
plainly than in Romans 14:

> For to this end Christ both died, and rose, and revived, that
> he might be Lord both of the dead and living.
> > Romans 14:9

Lordship is why Christ died. Restoring God as the Sovereign
in the heart of man is what the gospel is all about. In Christ's sacrifice,

the penalty levied under God's authority was paid, and in repentance from sin, allegiance to God is restored. Why else did Paul proclaim salvation by calling on the "Lord" instead of the "Savior" in Romans 10:9? Does this mean the sinner must make an itemized list of every area of his life and surrender it over to God? No. That would certainly qualify as adding works to the gospel. And it is important in making this point that the reader does not confuse yielding to God and submitting to Him in repentance with the Roman Catholic doctrine of confession. The Bible never describes a checklist of things a sinner must confess and yield to Christ. But on the other hand, if the Holy Ghost is working on the heart about a particular area, and the sinner refuses to give it over to God, he is not a candidate for grace. God requires an unconditional surrender, but this is not to say that the surrender agreement must list each and every area of the sinner's life. Repentance is not a negotiation or an itemization; it is an attitude. And this changed attitude produces a saint, loyal to a new Master and sanctified to good works.

Yet antinomian preachers like Jack Hyles and those who have come after him undermine the gospel by throwing out this change of allegiance and repentance from sin. And in so doing, they demonstrate that this issue really does boil down to an authority problem. They disregard God's Law as supreme. They are not interested in Jesus Christ as Lord, but only as Savior. Like the multitudes who followed Jesus only for the miracles and free meals, the Antinomians are only interested in a humanistic Jesus who will spare their hide a scorching while leaving their lifestyle intact. No clearer statement to this effect can be found than that blasphemously spoken by Jack Hyles in his sermon, "Worthy Is the Lamb:"

Repentance is not a negotiation or an itemization; it is an attitude.

> Somebody said, "You trust in Jesus, you can go to heaven."
> No, you can't. You trust Him as a king, and you'll die and
> go to hell. You trust Him as a priest, and you'll die and go to
> hell. You trust Him as your Lord, you'll die and go to hell.
> You don't need a king; you need a sacrifice.[202]

And yet the entire book of Hebrews was written to teach trusting in Jesus as King, Priest, and Lord. All of history will one day culminate in a moment in which "every tongue should confess that Jesus Christ is Lord, to the glory of God the Father."[203] Because that is the work of the gospel: restoring humanity to God. And those who do not repent of their rebellion in this life will do so in the next.

The antinomian heresy teaches that sin, far from being a heinous trespass against God's holy law, is merely "missing the mark," as though the sinner is trying his best but just didn't quite measure up. Rebellion against God is not that serious to the Antinomian, and therefore it makes no sense to them for the gospel to vanquish it. Yet that is precisely what the Bible states in I John:

> Whosoever committeth sin transgresseth also the law: for
> sin is the transgression of the law.
> And ye know that he was manifested to take away our sins;
> and in him is no sin.
> Whosoever abideth in him sinneth not: whosoever sinneth
> hath not seen him, neither known him.
> Little children, let no man deceive you: he that doeth
> righteousness is righteous, even as he is righteous.
> He that committeth sin is of the devil; for the devil sinneth
> from the beginning. For this purpose the Son of God was
> manifested, that he might destroy the works of the devil.[204]

Let there be no confusion. Sin is the transgression of the law, and Christ died to take away that sin and to destroy the works of the devil. Those who have repented of their sin and turned their allegiance over to God in their hearts are now new creatures. No longer the monsters of iniquity spawned from Adam's tainted bloodline, saints are now free to be children of God and to walk in holiness and sanctification. Having repented not only from unbelief, but from whatever sin stood between them and God, and having submitted to the Lord, the saint is rescued from the power of sin and free to serve a new Master. The war is over. At the point of regeneration, the sinner lays down his weapons of rebellion, submits to King Jesus, and receives a full pardon. Sin has no more dominion.

Chapter 8

OBJECTIONS REFUTED

Ye have wearied the Lord with your words. Yet ye say,
Wherein have we wearied him? When ye say, Every
one that doeth evil is good in the sight of the Lord,
and he delighteth in them; or, Where is the God of
judgment?

Malachi 2:17

It would be tragic to spend a life arguing past a position, rather than against it, and never make an impact on the opposing side. In the interest of intellectual honesty and profitable communication, great pains have been taken to understand just what those in the antinomian camp actually teach and believe and how best to refute their arguments rather than the arguments we think they espouse. Here, the ten most common antinomian objections to our doctrine will be listed with a sound refutation following.

It is the premise of this book that repentance is a change of heart and mind regarding actions, committed or intended, resulting in a change of course. In Scripture, the term almost never refers to turning from a belief, and almost always refers to turning from an action – and in the context of the gospel, that action is almost always sin. The turn away from sin that is required for salvation is only an intention and, of necessity, includes a turn to belief in Christ. Repentance is in no way meritorious, and the salvation that results is a work completely wrought by God. Unfortunately, those who disagree with repentance from sin in the gospel often fail to understand our doctrine, whereas some hate it precisely because they do understand it. We shall now consider what they have to say about repentance from sin and soundly refute their most cherished objections against it.

Objection 1: There are many gospel/salvation passages in the Bible that mention only faith and not repentance.

It is true that many passages referring to salvation or the gospel make no mention of repentance. As was discussed in Chapter 6, repentance and faith are intimately connected and cannot be separated. They are two sides of the same coin. The sinner who repents truly believes. And the sinner who truly believes repents. As evangelist, James Stewart, wrote:

> Faith is the open hand, relatively to the gift; repentance is the same hand, relatively, not only to the gift but more especially to the dagger that is flung from it...Repentance looks within, faith looks above.[205]

But this objection can also be turned on its head. What about the many gospel/salvation passages in the Bible that reference only repentance and completely omit any mention of faith or belief? This objection blows up on this one point – that there are many passages that mention no faith just as there are passages that mention no repentance. And this only underscores our point that the two are wrapped up in one another and totally inseparable. There is not one mention of faith in these gospel/salvation passages:

> But go ye and learn what that meaneth, I will have mercy, and not sacrifice: for I am not come to call the righteous, but sinners to repentance.
>
> Matthew 9:13

> John did baptize in the wilderness, and preach the baptism of repentance for the remission of sins.
>
> Mark 1:4

When Jesus heard it, he saith unto them, They that are whole have no need of the physician, but they that are sick: I came not to call the righteous, but sinners to repentance.

Mark 2:17

And they went out, and preached that men should repent.

Mark 6:12

I say unto you, that likewise joy shall be in heaven over one sinner that repenteth, more than over ninety and nine just persons, which need no repentance.

Luke 15:7

And that repentance and remission of sins should be preached in his name among all nations, beginning at Jerusalem.

Luke 24:47

Repent ye therefore, and be converted, that your sins may be blotted out, when the times of refreshing shall come from the presence of the Lord.

Acts 3:19

This objection blows up on this one point – that there are many passages that mention no faith just as there are passages that mention no repentance.

Him hath God exalted with his right hand to be a Prince and a Saviour, for to give repentance to Israel, and forgiveness of sins.

Acts 5:31

When they heard these things, they held their peace, and glorified God, saying, Then hath God also to the Gentiles granted repentance unto life.

Acts 11:18

But shewed first unto them of Damascus, and at Jerusalem, and throughout all the coasts of Judaea, and then to the

Gentiles, that they should repent and turn to God, and do works meet for repentance.

Acts 26:20

For godly sorrow worketh repentance to salvation not to be repented of: but the sorrow of the world worketh death.

II Corinthians 7:10

The Lord is not slack concerning his promise, as some men count slackness; but is longsuffering to us-ward, not willing that any should perish, but that all should come to repentance.

II Peter 3:9

Objection 2: The Philippian jailor did not repent.

As was briefly discussed in Chapter 2, the Bible teaches law to the proud and grace to the humble. In James 4:6, the Bible says, "God resisteth the proud, but giveth grace unto the humble." The Philippian jailor was already in a penitent and humble state. The story does not record many details, but the very fact that he approached the preacher with the question, "What must I do to be saved," speaks volumes about his attitude. As mentioned previously, there are many gospel/salvation passages that do not record repentance, and there are many that do not record belief. This passage does not stand alone in the Word of God, and it should not make up the entirety of our soteriology.

Furthermore, this story is consistent with the principle of law to the proud and grace to the humble. Because the Philippian jailor was not lifted up with self-righteous pride and was reaching out for salvation, grace was immediately bestowed. He was reaching out with the open hand of faith, a hand that did not hold a dagger of rebellion in it.

Antinomians often point out that this new convert took Paul and Silas back to prison the next morning and thus could not have been submitted to Christ's Lordship. Yet this only underscores that new converts do not always know the specifics of applying their new faith and allegiance in their everyday life. This is especially true in matters of government. It can be very confusing – especially for a Christian saved less than 24 hours – to reconcile the commands of a godless government with the commands of God. Lordship does not require perfect application, only perfect submission. But it should be noted that the passage does actually record evidence of submission to God's laws (and thus repentance and surrender). According to Acts 16:33, he immediately obeyed the first commandment God gives to those who are born again. The passage says he "was baptized, he and all his, straightway."

Objection 3: No one can repent of each and every sin they have committed.

As was pointed out in Chapter 5, the doctrine of repentance from sin is not to be confused with the Roman Catholic doctrine of confession. And thus, this objection is a straw man. The Antinomian here accuses the biblical gospel preacher of teaching something he does not actually teach. Of course, the gospel does not require the sinner to make a laundry list of each and every sin they have ever committed and confess it individually to God. I am not aware of a single fundamentalist preacher who teaches this. And yet the Bible does command sinners to turn from all their sins:

> Because he considereth, and turneth away from all his transgressions that he hath committed, he shall surely live, he shall not die.
> Yet saith the house of Israel, The way of the Lord is not equal. O house of Israel, are not my ways equal? are not your ways unequal?
> Therefore I will judge you, O house of Israel, every one according to his ways, saith the Lord God. Repent, and turn yourselves from all your transgressions; so iniquity shall not be your ruin.
>
> Ezekiel 18:28-30

Why? Certainly, the Bible does not mean the sinner should rattle off a list of sins in order to deserve grace. But Scripture does insist that nothing can be held back. If there is anything the sinner refuses to yield to God, he cannot receive grace, for he is not exercising true faith in the Redeemer. The sinner must repent from a past, present, and future of sin in the sense that he

Of course the gospel does not require the sinner to make a laundry list of each and every sin they have ever committed and confess it individually to God.

rejects sin as a concept. He will not even understand this turn in full at the moment of salvation, most likely, but unless the turn is made, he will not see heaven. Consider the story of the rich, young ruler who came to Jesus and asked how he might be saved. The Bible records that he kept the commandments and was upright – but Jesus pointed to the one, single sin He knew the young man would not want to give up: his materialistic greed. Rather than tell the ruler to just believe, even though the passage says Jesus loved this young man,[206] Christ refused to cheapen the gospel and refused to grant him eternal life, because of that one, solitary sin he would not repent of.

Objection 4: You do not have to make Jesus Lord of every area of your life to be saved.

This is yet another straw man fallacy. The premise of this book does not state that the sinner has to take a mental inventory of every facet of his life, without forgetting a single area, and consciously yield it to God. As briefly discussed in Chapter 7, that would be earning salvation. This is not what repentance from sin entails. But repentance *does* require the sinner to yield completely to God's will, His lordship, and His law, as a whole. In other words, the treasonous sinner must come to the surrender summit with no reservations or conditions. He must confess Christ as Lord in unconditional surrender, purposing to go with God no matter what. He does not tell God that he will keep most of God's commandments and retain only his materialistic greed like the rich, young ruler did. That would be bargaining with God and trying to affect his own salvation. God is not interested in a bargain, and He wants the sinner to confess Jesus – not as friend, buddy, boyfriend, or man upstairs, but as "Lord:"

> That if thou shalt confess with thy mouth the Lord Jesus, and shalt believe in thine heart that God hath raised him from the dead, thou shalt be saved.
>
> Romans 10:9

Indeed, this is the whole point of the gospel, for sinners to turn their allegiance away from idols and to God:

> For to this end Christ both died, and rose, and revived, that he might be Lord both of the dead and living.
>
> Romans 14:9

> For they themselves shew of us what manner of entering in we had unto you, and how ye turned to God from idols to serve the living and true God;
>
> I Thessalonians 1:9

In the Old Testament, we read of a story that illustrates this principle. Achan went in with the Hebrews to destroy Jericho, but God commanded them to sanctify the entire city to God and reserve nothing to themselves. Achan was not required to take an inventory of those things he destroyed for God, but he was required to keep nothing back. But because he reserved to himself just a few accursed things, he was sentenced to death. Likewise, the sinner must not come to Jesus with accursed reservations or conscious refusal to yield on a particular matter. True faith and repentance demand that he unreservedly confess Jesus as His Lord.

Objection 5: If repentance from sin saves, then returning to sin would cause you to lose that salvation.

The Antinomian often fails to understand this doctrine or simply refuses to consider it and therefore argues past it quite frequently. This objection is yet another straw man because we do not teach that repentance saves. And in truth, faith does not save, either. Ultimately, it is God's grace that saves. The Bible does teach that true salvation that changes a person into a child of God cannot be lost, and therefore, any doctrine which could undermine this blessed security of the believer should be questioned. But biblical repentance does not undermine security any more than faith does.

The Antinomian reasons that, if repenting from sin saves a person, the moment that person fails to live in repentance, slips up, and goes back to that sin, he is no longer saved. But what about faith? The Antinomian skeptic pits repentance and faith against one another as diametrically opposed alternatives, and is therefore faced with the same problem. If faith, instead of repentance from sin, saves the sinner, then the moment that person doubts or turns back to serving false gods, he would lose his salvation, according to their logic. And so this objection blows up as hypocritical because the Antinomian has the same problem we do. In fact, most Antinomians will admit on the basis of I Thessalonians 1:9, which commands repentance from idols, that the sinner must repent from idolatry to be saved. But what if that saved person then goes back to their idols and no longer has faith in Jesus? According to this logic, that person would lose their salvation! Granted, some Antinomians will attempt to save face by insisting that a truly saved person could never turn back to unbelief or idols – but the Bible specifically warns Christians from doing just that in I John 5:21, so it is certainly possible.

Fortunately, neither faith nor repentance is what ultimately saves – God's grace saves. Repentance and faith are merely the means by which God's free and everlasting grace is administered. Notice the word, "through," in the following verse:

For by grace are ye saved through faith; and that not of yourselves: it is the gift of God:

Ephesians 2:9

When we open our hand, formerly clenched around the dagger of sin, and extend it in faith that it will be filled with grace, God saves us solely by His own might. Our faith and repentance do not save or keep us saved; they merely open the door for God's grace to get through.

Fortunately, neither faith nor repentance are what ultimately save – God's grace saves. Repentance and faith are merely the means by which God's free and everlasting grace is administered.

Objection 6: God repents more than anyone in the Bible, so repentance cannot mean turning from sin, since God has no sin.

This was discussed extensively in Chapter 5, but it is worth including a brief recap here because this is such a commonly used objection. It is true that God is said to repent more than any other one person is said to repent in Scripture. This is not surprising, however. God is the central person in the Bible, mentioned from cover to cover on nearly every page. It would stand to reason that He would be associated with almost everything more than any other single person in the Bible. Nonetheless, the Antinomian considers this reason enough to believe the word has little to do with turning from sin and more to do with turning from a belief system. This could not be further from the truth.

The word, *repent*, in all its variations, occurs 112 times in 105 verses in the *King James Bible*, all of which are analyzed in Appendix A. The first mention is of God turning from an action He had done, and the last mention is of people turning from sinful actions they had done. The overwhelming majority of the mentions between refer to a turn from or regret for a (typically negative) action – typically sin – whether committed or intended. Paradoxically, the Bible at times says that God is not a man that He should repent.[207] But what these verses refer to is that God does not change His covenants or promises; He only changes his attitudes and actions. So in many places we find God repenting from some action He either committed or intended to commit. He does not repent for who He is or what He believes. And this is consistent with our definition: a change of mind and heart regarding actions, committed or intended, resulting in a change of course.

The statistics do not lie. The Bible defines its own terms. There is absolutely no basis in Scripture for the groundless theory that

In many places we find God repenting from some action He either committed or intended to commit. He does not repent for who He is or what He believes.

"repent" in Scripture means only or primarily to turn from unbelief to belief or that it has nothing to do with actually turning from sinful actions. Yes, God repents from actions, and thus repentance means to turn from actions. And in the context of the gospel extended to mankind, those actions are sins. In fact, of all the mentions of *repent* in Scripture, approximately half refer to turning from sin, and most of the remaining half refer to God turning from actions, not beliefs.

Objection 7: The phrase, "repent of your sins" never appears in the Bible.

This objection really is quite silly. As was briefly discussed in Chapter 2, the rationale is essentially that the doctrine of repentance from sin can be thrown out simply because the exact phrase, "repent of your sins," does not appear in Scripture. Unless those exact words appear in that exact order, many Antinomians will not believe that salvation requires repentance from sins. They are seemingly unaware of synonyms. There are several places in the Bible that tell people to repent of their sins to be saved, but the wording is only slightly different. You see, the English language is a vast language and affords the writer numerous ways to say the same thing. Here is one such example in which the phrase appears as "forsake his way:"

> Seek ye the Lord while he may be found, call ye upon him while he is near:
> Let the wicked forsake his way, and the unrighteous man his thoughts: and let him return unto the Lord, and he will have mercy upon him; and to our God, for he will abundantly .
> pardon.
>
> Isaiah 55:6-7

A full analysis of this passage was provided in Chapter 6 to demonstrate that this is most definitely a salvation passage and does not refer to working for physical salvation. It most emphatically speaks of a turn of heart and mind away from sins and to the eternal Savior.

Another such passage only a few chapters away uses the term, "turn from transgression." Notice it speaks prophetically of the coming "Redeemer" and is also not a reference to temporal, physical salvation in exchange for works:

> And the Redeemer shall come to Zion, and unto them that turn from transgression in Jacob, saith the LORD.
>
> Isaiah 59:20

In Ezekiel 18, this command appears multiple times, often very close to the exact phrase the Antinomian requires. Throughout the chapter, the Bible says things like, "turn from all his sins," "return from his ways," "turneth away from his wickedness," and "Repent...

from all your transgressions." Granted, this passage is primarily speaking of physical salvation, and yet there is a spiritual application, as well. At the very least, the skeptic must admit that it destroys the objection that the Bible never tells people to turn from their sins or repent of their sins. The Bible may not use the exact phrase, but it certainly says the same thing in many places, often within the context of spiritual salvation.

In the New Testament, the Bible records Peter telling a false convert to repent of his sins in very clear, synonymous terms. Judging from the context, this man was only interested in Christianity for the monetary gain he could derive from it, and so we must conclude that Peter was urging Him to ask God for eternal forgiveness, and not merely referencing I John 1:9-style confession of the believer. In fact, Peter indicates quite clearly that the man is not saved at all, insisting, "Thou hast neither part nor lot in this matter."[208] He tells Simon the Sorcerer:

> Repent therefore of this thy wickedness, and pray God, if
> perhaps the thought of thine heart may be forgiven thee.
>
>   Acts 8:22

Like Simon the Sorcerer, many Antinomians will overlook the phrase, "repent therefore of this thy wickedness," simply because they seek a physical salvation that does not interfere with their sin and spares them from the pain of hell. But the Bible rebukes sinners like Simon, commanding them to repent of their sins. Yet they pretend these commands simply do not exist, seeking instead for a cheaper gospel. Simon's humanistic response to Peter's rebuke is the easy-believeist's anthem:

> Pray ye to the Lord for me, that none of these things which
> ye have spoken come upon me.[209]

Objection 8: Repentance is Jewish.

While much could be said about the dangers of *Dispensationalism* – the view that the Bible is divided into different messages for different times and peoples – and while there are differing shades of this belief system, Dispensationalism is a subject for another time. However, since many Dispensationalists discount repentance for Gentiles in this New Testament age and apply it only to the Jews, this objection is worth addressing in brief. Many Dispensationalists believe God gave the Jews of the Old Testament and the Gentiles of the New Testament completely separate gospels, the former requiring the work of repentance and the latter requiring only faith. To separate repentance out from faith is completely contrary to the Bible, which often uses the terms interchangeably because they are so intimately connected in the work of regeneration. And to preach works for salvation in any age, besides grossly overestimating the ability of man to impress God, is to mock the perfect work of Calvary in all its completeness and simplicity. Calvary was not an asterisk in the plan of redemption, but rather its crowning element, the very substance of God's relation to man.

Nevertheless, are scriptures mentioning repentance only given to Jews in the Old Testament? Paris Reidhead recalled his being trained in this erroneous belief system only to find the truth from – ironically – one of the most prolific Dispensationalists of the 20th century, Harry Ironside, the renowned pastor of Moody Church in Chicago. Reidhead writes:

> We were told that "repentance" has nothing to do with the "Age of Grace," that repentance was for the Jews... Remarkably, it was another dispensationalist who set me straight...You see, dispensationalists took the Law of God away from preparing hearts for conviction and repentance... they succeeded in disarming the Holy Spirit of the only instrument He ever provided Himself to prepare men for grace.[210]

In making repentance a uniquely Jewish and outdated doctrine, the dispensational Antinomian removes the schoolteacher of the law from the equation. Antinomianism disarms the Holy Ghost of this powerful tool with which to show sinners their need for a Savior. In the absence of the law, soul winners are left trying to sell a gospel that is not needed or valued, often resorting to cheap sales tricks and gimmicks to close the deal. The Bible is quite clear on the matter. We have only to look at the many references commanding all men to repent to see that repentance is not unique to the Jews of old. The great Dispensationalist, Harry Ironside, himself, comments:

> If others object on the ground that Peter was the Apostle of the circumcision and that there is a distinction to be drawn between the message to the Jew and that to the Gentile, I would point to the fact that, in the house of Cornelius with a Gentile audience before him, his message is of exactly the same character as when he is preaching to his Jewish brethren after the flesh…he was addressing a truly repentant group, as Cornelius' attitude clearly attested…When his brethren heard the whole story "they held their peace, and glorified God, saying, Then hath God also to the Gentiles granted repentance unto life" (v. 18).[211]

Of course, many dispensational Antinomians would argue that this story recorded in the book of Acts – or any of the other repentance passages in Acts – cannot be used to teach the doctrine of repentance, because Acts is a transitional book and not doctrinal. However, the Bible clearly states that "All scripture is given by inspiration of God, and is profitable for doctrine."[212] The dispensational antinomian retort to this reference is that comparing Scripture with Scripture reveals not all Scripture is profitable for doctrine, since some passages in Leviticus, for example, clearly do not apply to the New Testament saint. However, this is to call God a liar and overlook the fact that even passages directed to Old Testament Jews can, in fact, teach doctrine to New Testament saints. Besides, just what Scriptural reference should we compare with Acts to determine that the entire book is off limits for doctrine? Where is it decreed in Scripture that Acts is off limits for doctrinal instruction? Charles Spurgeon, in a sermon given March of 1855, called out this mishandling of the Bible:

> Strange that there should be men so vile as to use the penknife of Jehoiakim to cut passages out of the word, because they are unpalatable. O ye who dislike certain portions of Holy Writ, rest assured that your taste is corrupt, and that God will not stay for you (sic) little opinion. Your dislike is the very reason why God wrote it, because you out (sic) not to be suited; you have no right to be pleased. God wrote what you do not like; he wrote the truth...Blessed Bible! thou art all truth.[213]

Repentance can be found throughout both testaments, proclaimed to both Jews and Gentiles. Sin must be repented of, no matter your ethnicity. Since Paul was the apostle to the Gentiles, let his words speak authoritatively on the matter, how he taught repentance to both Jews and Greeks (Gentiles) alike:

"All scripture is given by inspiration of God, and is profitable for doctrine."

> And how I kept back nothing that was profitable unto you, but have shewed you, and have taught you publicly, and from house to house,
> Testifying both to the Jews, and also to the Greeks, repentance toward God, and faith toward our Lord Jesus Christ.
>
> Acts 20:20-21

Objection 9: Unbelief is the only sin that damns.

This subject was dealt with in detail in Chapter 7, but for convenience, we shall summarize the most popular passages used to make this argument and the biblical way to respond. Below are the three passages most used to teach that only unbelief sends people to hell, and not their sins. After each passage will follow a brief comment of rebuttal.

> He that believeth on him is not condemned: but he that believeth not is condemned already, because he hath not believed in the name of the only begotten Son of God.
>
> John 3:18

Antinomians love to cite this passage, because it seems to teach that sinners are condemned because they have not believed in the name of Jesus. But if they would read more closely, they would find the verse plainly says that sinners who do not believe were *already* condemned. The Bible teaches that sinners are damned for their sins and are therefore condemned before they ever have a chance to believe or not believe in the good news of the gospel.

> He that believeth on the Son hath everlasting life: and he that believeth not the Son shall not see life; but the wrath of God abideth on him.
>
> John 3:36

This passage simply does not comment on the matter, although Antinomians often cite it as if it does. It merely says those who believe have everlasting life and those who do not believe do not have everlasting life. As hinted at by the last phrase of the verse, their condemnation abides on them from the time of their first sin, as multiple scriptures attest. Nowhere does this passage contradict other passages and teach that unbelief is what damns the sinner.

> And when he is come, he will reprove the world of sin, and of righteousness, and of judgment:
> Of sin, because they believe not on me;
>
> John 16:8-9

Pastor Steven Anderson of Tempe, Arizona and many other Antinomians will leap upon this passage as though the judgment of verse 8 only comes because of the unbelief in verse 9. Once again, however, the passage simply does not say that. Language is a beautiful gift from God, and we should be faithful stewards of this gift, not skimming over passages and then making deep theological conclusions based only on the general feeling we get from reading them. Upon thoughtful, deliberate review, we find this verse actually teaches that the Comforter (verse 7) will reprove the world for their *sin* (not just unbelief) – which is the exact opposite of what Anderson's Antinomians pretend this passage teaches! So why does verse 9 include the phrase, "because they believe not on me?" The answer is quite simply that God judges people on one of two criteria: Christ's sinless record, if they have believed in Him, or their own sinful record, if they have not believed. They can either answer for their own works, or they can trust in Christ's righteousness and never be judged on their own works, but rather only on His. Consider these passages that tell us sin is what brings the wrath of God upon sinners and that sinners are judged in the end according to their works:

> And I saw the dead, small and great, stand before God; and the books were opened: and another book was opened, which is the book of life: and the dead were judged out of those things which were written in the books, according to their works.
> And the sea gave up the dead which were in it; and death and hell delivered up the dead which were in them: and they were judged every man according to their works.
>   Revelation 20:12-13

> For the wages of sin is death; but the gift of God is eternal life through Jesus Christ our Lord.
>   Romans 6:23

> Mortify therefore your members which are upon the earth; fornication, uncleanness, inordinate affection, evil

God judges people on one of two criteria: Christ's sinless record, if they have believed in Him, or their own sinful record, if they have not believed.

concupiscence, and covetousness, which is idolatry:
For which things' sake the wrath of God cometh on the children of disobedience:

Colossians 3:5-6

For this ye know, that no whoremonger, nor unclean person, nor covetous man, who is an idolater, hath any inheritance in the kingdom of Christ and of God.

Let no man deceive you with vain words: for because of these things cometh the wrath of God upon the children of disobedience.

Ephesians 5:5-6

Objection 10: Repentance from sin is a work.

Although this accusation has been dealt with in part throughout this book, it constitutes the most central and common objection raised by the Antinomians and deserves an in-depth, detailed response. Every Antinomian will make this claim. It will be the first and primary attack made on the gospel of repentance, and it will be assumed as truth throughout any discussion on the issue. Antinomian logic posits that turning from sin is a work, and therefore, it is adding works to the gospel to say repentance from sin is part of the gospel command. From this launch pad, the Antinomian can then argue all of the aforementioned objections. In his mind, all who preach repentance stand for works salvation, whereas he is the defender of grace through faith. And while many Antinomians are genuinely confused and sincere in their desire to attack what they perceive as a corruption of the gospel, many others specifically hate bringing sin into the picture because it shines the light on their unconverted, unholy lives. Both types of Antinomian must be shown the truth that repentance from sin is not a works gospel but the biblical gospel.

Without a doubt, the holy-grail verse to which Antinomians will always refer when arguing that repentance from sin is a work is this:

> And God saw their works, that they turned from their evil way; and God repented of the evil, that he had said that he would do unto them; and he did it not.
>
>   Jonah 3:10

Because the verse seems to refer to turning from their evil way as "works," the Antinomian forever equates repentance from sin with earning salvation. Yet there are several observations that will show this to be categorically false, the first of which is that the Bible calls faith a work, too. The multitudes once asked Jesus what they had to do to be saved, and both they and He referred to a work:

> Then said they unto him, What shall we do, that we might work the works of God?
> Jesus answered and said unto them, This is the work of God, that ye believe on him whom he hath sent.
>
>   John 6:28-29

Should we then conclude that faith is adding works to the gospel? Is grace only free if it happens to us completely irrespective of our reception of it? After all, believing is something one does, and therefore, it could be said that doing something is necessary for salvation. Believing is technically a work just like repentance is – the Bible tells us so. But is it meritorious? Can we earn salvation by it? This is the distinction that should be made. The question is not whether one must do something to be saved, but whether one can earn salvation. The sinner must believe in Jesus, repent, and call upon the name of the Lord, but these things the sinner does do not earn salvation. In fact, the Bible says God gives these things to us.

Historically, church creeds and statements of faith have referred to faith and repentance as *twin graces*, given by God. Notice in verse 29 of this passage, Jesus identifies faith as a work "of God." If God gives us the work of faith, it is not of ourselves but a gift,[214] and we cannot earn salvation with it. And preaching that it is required for salvation is not adding works to the gospel. Likewise, the Bible also tells us in the below passages that God gives us repentance just as He does faith:

> Him hath God exalted with his right hand to be a Prince and a Saviour, for to give repentance to Israel, and forgiveness of sins.
>
> Acts 5:31

> Then hath God also to the Gentiles granted repentance unto life.
>
> Acts 11:18b

Strictly defined, repentance is a gift of God, and not a meritorious work by which we earn salvation. But it does produce works. And this is why God could see the change in the Ninevites, because their heart repentance resulted in a chance of action. And this is also why John the Baptist preached that his converts should not only repent but also produce works "meet for repentance"[215] or suitable to repentance. Works

Believing is technically a work just like repentance is – the Bible tells us so. But is it meritorious? Can we earn salvation by it? This is the distinction that should be made.

always follow saving repentance. And just as we refer to both the source of light and the ray of light it produces as "light," so we can refer to both the turn of mind and the change of life it produces as "repentance."

If repentance from sin is a meritorious work that earns something, that which it earns could never be described as "mercy." And yet that is precisely what the Bible calls that which is given to those who repent:

> He that covereth his sins shall not prosper: but whoso confesseth and forsaketh them shall have mercy.
>
> Proverbs 28:13

For some reason, Antinomians often throw this verse out because they believe it is not referring to salvation. While this is certainly up for debate, the point is valid regardless of the context. If forsaking sins is a meritorious work, then those who do it would receive a *wage*, not "mercy." Yet here the Bible demonstrates that turning from sin is not earning anything and will incur mercy from God.

Consider the story of Naaman, the leper, who went to Elisha for healing. This story is quite obviously a type or picture of the sinner who goes to God for healing from his sin disease. And yet the man of God gave Naaman something to do. He did not tell him to pay him for the gift of healing (in fact, when Gahazi accepted a gift from Naaman, he was cursed for it); that would have spoiled the picture of free grace. But he was nevertheless given a task to complete. He was to dip in the Jordan River seven times and be healed. Was washing in the river an action? Of course. But it in no way earned his healing. In fact, we see the contrast between meritorious works and the simplicity of obeying the gospel when Naaman's servants asked:

> My father, if the prophet had bid thee do some great thing, wouldest thou not have done it? how much rather then, when he saith to thee, Wash, and be clean?
>
> II Kings 5:13

In obeying this simple command to wash and be clean, Naaman exercised faith that it would work and that he would be healed. Likewise, the sinner who repents of sin exercises faith that God will cleanse and save him. In this way, God has outlined certain requirements or prerequisites for grace. These are in no way meritorious, yet they are to be obeyed. He who does not trust in Jesus will not be saved. And he who does not repent from his sin will not be saved. Both can be said to be works or actions, but neither can be said to be meritorious or earning salvation.

To further illustrate the principle of meeting certain conditions for salvation, imagine you hear of a shoe-company giveaway coming up. You are told that anyone who drops what they are doing on the first of next month and comes down to the local store wearing red, the company's brand color, will receive a brand-new pair of designer shoes for free. So when the first of the month rolls around, you drop what you are doing, head down to the shoe store wearing a red shirt, and claim your free pair of designer shoes. The next day, a friend comments on your new shoes and asks how you got them. Do you tell your friend you earned them? Of course not. You would most likely exclaim, "I got these for *free!*" Dropping your plans for the day did not equate to earning them. Going to the store did not equate to earning them. Wearing a red shirt did not equate to earning them. This was a giveaway. You were given those shoes for free. But there were certain conditions you had to meet.

Repentance does not save any more than faith does. The Bible says only grace saves us. But we receive that grace by repenting of our sins and putting our trust in Jesus. Without one, you cannot have the other. Martin Luther, in his original disputations against the ancient Antinomians, affirmed this very thing:

> Therefore justification certainly follows upon contrition, not as an effect of contrition, but of grace, that is, grace is the efficient cause of justification, not contrition.[216]

Harry Ironside had this to add:

> Repentance is not opposed to grace; it is the recognition
> of the need of grace…Yet there are not wanting professed
> preachers of grace who, like the antinomians of old, decry
> the necessity of repentance lest it seem to invalidate the
> freedom of grace. As well might one object to a man's
> acknowledgment of illness when seeking help and healing
> from a physician, on the ground that all he needed was a
> doctor's prescription.[217]

It is not adding works to the gospel to require the sinner to reach out his hand and receive the free gift. It is not adding works to the gospel to require the sinner to acknowledge his depravity and need for a Savior. It is not adding works to the gospel to require the sinner to believe on the Lord Jesus Christ.

So how about Jonah 3:10? Does it matter that it calls turning from sin a work? We have seen how faith is also referred to as a work, how both faith and repentance are works wrought in us by God, how the work is merely a precondition and does not equate to earning anything, and how those who repent receive mercy rather than wages. But there is one more thing to consider as it pertains to Jonah 3:10. What God saw was the same kind of work described in the book of James – the resulting change of action that comes from a change of intention or attitude. We have maintained throughout this book that repentance is a change of heart and mind regarding actions, committed or intended, resulting in a change of course. It is that change of heart and mind that is a prerequisite for grace. But it was the resulting change of course that is referred to in Jonah 3:10. Therefore it is invalid to object that repentance from sin is a work, because this kind of repentance refers to an intention or attitude.

The Bible tells us that just looking with lust is adultery[218] and hating someone is murder.[219] In other words, God counts the mere intention to do something as though it had been done. This is a striking parallel to the gospel. The Bible says God counted the faith of Abraham for righteousness.[220] He did not do works of righteousness, yet it was counted as though he had. When God told Abraham to sacrifice his son, Isaac, He stopped him from going through with it. He only wanted to see his intention. Likewise, the intention to live for God and not for self is counted for righteousness. God grants grace freely, not to those who try to earn it or buy God off, but to those who humbly yield to the Gospel command, dropping their sinful dagger of rebellion, intending to cease from sin, and extending their open hand to God, fully believing they will receive that which they could never earn.

Chapter 9

THE NEW BIRTH

Therefore we are buried with him by baptism into death: that like as Christ was raised up from the dead by the glory of the Father, even so we also should walk in newness of life.

Romans 6:4

The Church is dead. Numerous surveys and studies have been conducted over the past generation and found that the average church member does not pray, does not read his Bible, does not give, does not participate in evangelistic outreach, and often does not even attend services regularly. Pastors understand that only about five to ten percent of their congregation can be relied on for such things. Why? The great evangelist, A. W. Tozer, is quoted as having once said, "Among evangelical churches...probably no more than one out of ten know anything experientially about the new birth."[221] Something is very wrong in evangelical and fundamentalist churches today. False doctrine is prevalent, immorality is commonplace, and evangelistic fervor is nonexistent. Perhaps the problem comes down to the staggering fact that most church members have never been born again. Perhaps the overwhelming majority of self-identifying Christians – even in fundamentalist Baptist churches – today have entered the sheepfold some other way and are in fact imposters among us, as Christ warned about:

Verily, verily, I say unto you, He that entereth not by the
door into the sheepfold, but climbeth up some other way,
the same is a thief and a robber.
But he that entereth in by the door is the shepherd of the
sheep.

John 10:1-2

The Bible describes the new birth in far different terms than
what is heard in the average American church. It describes a process
of dying and reviving to new
life. And those who entered
into the fold without first being
crucified with Christ can never
experience the newness of life
that comes from walking in His
resurrection. We often speak
of being *saved*, and that is well
and good – regeneration does
save us from some things – but
this is not the essence of the
new birth. In fact, those who
experienced such a rebirth in the Bible did not refer to it as being
saved like we do. Paul referenced his conversion as that time when
God called him and revealed His Son in him.[222] He later described it
as a crucifixion:

> I am crucified with Christ: nevertheless I live; yet not I, but
> Christ liveth in me: and the life which I now live in the flesh
> I live by the faith of the Son of God, who loved me, and
> gave himself for me.
>
> Galatians 2:20

Indeed, Christ told His disciples on multiple occasions to take
up their cross and follow Him. He even told this to the rich, young
ruler who asked how to obtain eternal life.[223] Why all this talk about

Those who entered into the fold without first being crucified with Christ can never experience the newness of life that comes from walking in His resurrection.

death and execution? Keep in mind, Jesus had not been crucified by the Romans yet, so the cross had no religious overtones at this time. Yet Christ commanded His followers to die so they could be reborn. And just what is this death? In a word, repentance. Repentance is dying to self-will, self-righteousness, and self-ownership. But most church goers have never truly encountered such a dramatic loss. And thus, they have never had the opportunity to be reborn in the image of God's Son.

The Proper Presentation

There has been much debate about the proper way to present the gospel. Bible schools have created cookie-cutter programs that they insist upon for their students. Preachers have insisted upon certain techniques. And there is certainly a great need for the soul winner to use proper methods to convert the sinner. But care should also be taken to not simplify the gospel call too much. The new birth is not to be found in a formula. There is no magical sequence of instructions or a preferred prayer. One cannot simply profess repentance and faith and then be saved. The new birth is in many ways a mystery. It is a miracle of the Holy Ghost working within the sinner to bring about a spiritual crisis resulting in a change of direction and trust. And it is the height of arrogance for anyone to proclaim someone saved. Salvation is not a checklist to be completed in exchange for eternal life. Neither faith nor repentance should be viewed in this light. In his insightful book, *Finding the Reality of God*, Paris Reidhead observed:

> They have yet to realize that salvation is not a plan, not in scripture verses, not in ordinances, and not in a scheme of theology. Salvation is not a decision and not a pronouncement of an evangelist, a pastor, or a teacher.[224]

But we like our quick fixes and simple solutions. And so we have several generations of mass-produced Christians who come off the production line with a phony faith and a phony life to match it. Having been given the sanction and approval of their fellow Christians, these unregenerated tares are now twofold more the children of hell. They look down their noses at those who do not line up with their traditions of men and in the process make the commandments of God of none effect. Having never died to self, these false converts are guided by anything but the Holy Spirit. And what is more, they are our Sunday School teachers, pastors, best friends, and children. They are the quintessential Baptist or the church member in good standing. They have been packaged up and passed off as the real article, but they lack the stamp of authenticity. They do not have the Spirit of God living inside of them.

What a difference it would make if soul winners came back to the methods of the Bible, in which the fallow ground of hard hearts was first plowed up with the law and the holiness of God! How different our converts would be if they were first exposed to the harsh reality of their sin and prompted to respond in humble submission to the convicting work of the Spirit. How fervent our church members would be if they had ever been made to understand fully the depths of their own depravity and thus the depth of God's mercy in snatching them from their just deserts. Paul tells us in Romans, "by the law is the knowledge of sin."[225] But Antinomianism has snatched the law of God out of the hands of the Holy Ghost and left Him without His chosen tool of conviction unto life. Without the law of God, sinners do not sense the sinfulness of their sin or their need to be buried with Christ and resurrected with Him to a new life that does not resemble the old. Is there any surprise then that our church members act just like the world?

Some of the greatest sermons ever preached on the gospel dealt in very negative themes, because the gospel is first negative before it can be positive. The renowned colonial preacher, Jonathan Edwards, in his landmark sermon that fueled the Great Awakening in colonial America, *Sinners in the Hands of an Angry God*, stirred sinners to beg for mercy and come to God literally on their hands and knees. Observe the language of this gospel presentation:

> The God that holds you over the Pit of Hell, much as one holds a Spider, or some loathsome Insect, over the Fire, abhors you, and is dreadfully provoked; his Wrath towards you burns like Fire; he looks upon you as worthy of nothing else, but to be cast into the Fire; he is of purer Eyes than to bear to have you in his Sight; you are ten thousand Times so abominable in his Eyes as the most hateful venomous Serpent is in ours. You have offended him infinitely more than ever a stubborn Rebel did his Prince: and yet 'tis nothing but his Hand that holds you from falling into the Fire every Moment: 'Tis to be ascribed to nothing else, that you did not go to Hell the last Night;[226]

The new birth is in many ways a mystery. It is a miracle of the Holy Ghost working within the sinner to bring about a spiritual crisis resulting in a change of direction and trust.

Why the hellfire and brimstone? Why the negativity? Where is the message of love and warmth and acceptance so prevalent in the modern, antinomian gospel? Contrast this with the "Carl Hatch Squeeze" and positive gospel salesmanship of modern Antinomianism. Some might be tempted to argue that God is far more willing to save us than we are willing to be saved, that the gospel presentation should be about God's love and forgiveness. But what interest can the sinner have in God's forgiveness if he does not see himself as deplorable and wicked in the sight of a holy and wrathful God? If God is so willing to open His arms and embrace the rebel, so long as the rebel says the magic prayer or believes really hard, why did Jesus Christ intentionally withhold the good news of the gospel from a crowd of

hard-hearted people in the Gospel of Matthew? Heed the words of
the Master:

> Therefore speak I to them in parables: because they
> seeing see not; and hearing they hear not, neither do they
> understand.
> And in them is fulfilled the prophecy of Esaias, which saith,
> By hearing ye shall hear, and shall not understand; and
> seeing ye shall see, and shall not perceive:
> For this people's heart is waxed gross, and their ears are dull
> of hearing, and their eyes they have closed; lest at any time
> they should see with their eyes and hear with their ears, and
> should understand with their heart, and should be converted,
> and I should heal them.
>
>   Matthew 13:13-15

What strong words! What an unwilling Savior! The argument
that Christ is far more willing to save sinners than sinners are to be
saved is made in attempt to cheapen the gospel and advocate a positive
message of love and acceptance. Yet here, Jesus Christ admits to
hiding the good news from unrepentant sinners so that they will not
be saved. Why then do we insist upon giving the good news of the
gospel to those who are still entranced by their sin and self-love?

In his disputations with the ancient Antinomians, Martin Luther
argued that presenting the gospel of grace without the preaching of the
law is like a doctor prescribing medicine to a patient for a disease they
do not even know they have. He says:

> For how can he clarify and extol the benefits of Christ unless
> first our wretchedness and damage, into which we have
> fallen already from the beginning because of sin against the
> law, is brought into the sight of all?[227]

Likewise, Harry Ironside and many other holiness preachers
and authors have made this same analogy, comparing such an
erroneous presentation of the gospel to medicating someone without

an illness. This analogy comes straight from Jesus Christ. The Savior came to redeem mankind, but He placed much emphasis on the need for men to be made sinners before they could be made saints:

> And Jesus answering said unto them, They that are whole need not a physician; but they that are sick.
> I came not to call the righteous, but sinners to repentance.
>
> Luke 5:31-32

Matthew Henry wrote that repentance is a necessary preparative for the gospel and that the pain of confronting sin is necessary before the healing of the gospel can be administered:

> This repentance is a necessary duty, in obedience to the command of God (Acts. 17:30); and a necessary preparative and qualification for the comforts of the gospel of Christ. If the heart of man had continued upright and unstained, divine consolations might have been received without this painful operation preceding; but, being sinful, it must be first pained before it can be laid at ease, must labour before it can be at rest. The sore must be searched, or it cannot be cured.[228]

Consider the type or picture of Christ in Joseph, betrayed by his own brethren and forced into a life of slavery in Egypt. God eventually brought him to power as the second most powerful man in the country during a famine that brought his own brothers to beg grain of him, not knowing just who he was. Did Joseph immediately reveal himself and welcome them with the good news that he was Joseph and all their trials were ended? Quite the contrary. In fact, Joseph went out of his way to torment their spirits, even locking up one of them in prison, accusing them of theft, and alleging them to be foreign spies. He buffeted them with these anguishes until they produced that for which he sought: repentance. They confessed:

We are verily guilty concerning our brother, in that we saw the anguish of his soul, when he besought us, and we would not hear; therefore is this distress come upon us.[229]

The brothers were brought to sorrow for their guilt in what they did to Joseph. When presented with an opportunity that mirrored that which led them to sell their brother, Joseph, for gain, they chose the opposite course. Instead of allowing Benjamin to take the fall for the band of brothers, Judah offered himself up as a ransom for the life of his youngest brother. Only then did Joseph reveal the good news that he was their brother and that he had forgiven them. This is the proper order in presenting the gospel. This is how the mysterious power of the Holy Ghost can be brought to bear on the heart of the rebel. Sinners should be brought to godly sorrow, and only penitent sinners should be offered the positive message of forgiveness.

"This repentance is a necessary duty, in obedience to the command of God (Acts. 17:30); and a necessary preparative and qualification for the comforts of the gospel of Christ."

Be Ye Holy

When the Holy Spirit does a work in the heart of man, and he is turned from darkness unto light, the method and the words used to win him are secondary. This is not a formula or recipe. The new birth is a mysterious and miraculous transformation that converts a treasonous wretch into a child of the King. When God calls a person to repentance and faith, if they respond by dropping their dagger of sin and running to the Savior in full faith that He will pardon them, that is just what He does. But pardon is only part of the arrangement. That rebel is also made holy and is started down the path of sanctification.

Sure, he still has his old nature vying for dominion until Christ returns and our sinful bodies of flesh are glorified. But he also has something he never had before: a new nature. The supernatural work of God makes men holy. There will always be a struggle to reckon our sinful bodies of flesh dead to sin. But that person who truly believes on the Son is made a new creature – and that creature does not just do holy deeds, he *is* holy. John Wesley is quoted as having said:

> The new birth is that great change which God works in the soul, when He brings it into life and raises it from the death of sin to the life of righteousness. The new birth is the change wrought in the soul by the almighty Spirit of God, when that soul is created anew in Christ Jesus. The Spirit renews the soul of man after the image of God and adds to it righteousness and true holiness.[230]

The saint does not do good deeds because he has to or even because he wants to please God. The saint does good deeds because he *is* good. That person who has embraced the new birth and has been resurrected with Christ now has the Lord doing good from within him. He is now the vessel of righteousness used by the Master. Jesus not only gives us salvation, He *is* salvation. He is not only the way to new life, He is also the Truth and the new Life, itself.[231] The sinner who seeks salvation without the lordship of Jesus has missed the entire point. He is taking the Lord's name in vain to call himself a Christian without being controlled by the impulses of Christ. It is vanity to embrace salvation without holiness. Holiness is the very point of regeneration. And the Holy One of Israel is the Life which regenerates us.

This is the meaning of the book of James, in which the Bible tells us that our faith without works is dead.

That person who truly believes on the Son is made a new creature – and that creature does not just do holy deeds, he is holy.

The book even tells us that we are justified by works.[232] Does this contradict Paul, who wrote in Romans that we are justified by faith? Or does it rather point to the obedience to the gospel that results in saints who demonstrate their faith and new birth by continued obedience afterward? Matthew Henry comments on this passage, reconciling Paul with James and showing how justification makes men holy:

> When Paul says that a man is justified by faith, without the deeds of the law (Rom. 3:28), he plainly speaks of another sort of work than James does, but not of another sort of faith. Paul speaks of works wrought in obedience to the law of Moses, and before men's embracing the faith of the gospel; and he had to deal with those who valued themselves so highly upon those works that they rejected the gospel (as Rom. 10, at the beginning most expressly declares); but James speaks of works done in obedience to the gospel, and as the proper and necessary effects and fruits of sound believing in Christ Jesus. Both are concerned to magnify the faith of the gospel, as that which alone could save us and justify us; but Paul magnifies it by showing the insufficiency of any works of the law before faith, or in opposition to the doctrine of justification by Jesus Christ; James magnifies the same faith, by showing what are the genuine and necessary products and operations of it.[233]

So the point of James is not to teach obedience to the law to earn salvation, but rather to teach that those who have obeyed the gospel commands of repentance from sin and faith in the Savior will evidence this conversion by works. There is always that Antinomian who will interject that Christians can still backslide, and indeed they can and even do on rare occasions. The examples of Lot and Solomon are often proffered to show that God's saints can live like the devil's sinners. But these exceptions do not disprove the rule. In I John, the Bible says God's children live righteously, the devil's children live wickedly, and the whole point of the cross was to destroy sin:

He that committeth sin is of the devil; for the devil sinneth from the beginning. For this purpose the Son of God was manifested, that he might destroy the works of the devil... In this the children of God are manifest, and the children of the devil: whosoever doeth not righteousness is not of God, neither he that loveth not his brother.[234]

The point of James is not to teach obedience to the law to earn salvation, but rather to teach that those who have obeyed the gospel commands of repentance from sin and faith in the Savior will evidence this conversion by works.

That is the rule. The Word of God is clear on this matter. And while an occasional stumbling or even backsliding may occur in the life of the true believer, it is not the norm and should be considered exceptional. Indeed, more often than not, it is the mark of a false convert, a changling, a tare among wheat:

> They went out from us, but they were not of us; for if they had been of us, they would no doubt have continued with us: but they went out, that they might be made manifest that they were not all of us.
>
> I John 2:19

Is this passage not part of the Bible? Is it not authoritative? So why is it acceptable for so-called Christians to backslide or be dominated by sin? The Bible says it is a mark of the devil. These are not God's children. God's children are different. God's children are holy and love the things of God. They may stumble, but they will always get back up and quickly detest that sin that caused their stumbling. Those who do not love righteousness and holiness are not of God. Those who have not entered in at the strait gate of self-sacrificial repentance do not hate sin and can never be expected to rise above it or be zealous for good works.[235]

Abba, Father

The modern way of winning souls is to walk the sinner casually through the Romans Road, put forth the value proposition that being saved means going to heaven and getting out of hell, lead in a prayer, and then pronounce the sinner saved. What typically happens next is the sinner never shows up again, only attends church once or twice, or sticks around indefinitely while never doing anything for God or growing in maturity. These are all the marks of a sinner who still maintains his weapons of war against God, was interested in some fire insurance, and cannot be bothered with such trivialities as holiness and righteousness.

Many churchgoers live with nagging doubts about the salvation that was proclaimed over them by a preacher or soul winner. Rather than attempt to silence these doubts in young converts, we should recognize that assurance comes only from the Holy Ghost as the telltale confirmation of the new birth. If the law continues to burden the churchgoer and causes them to doubt their salvation, it may be that they lack the witness of God and are on their way to hell. Here is what the Bible states about this internal witness:

Assurance comes only from the Holy Ghost as the telltale confirmation of the new birth.

> But when the fulness of the time was come, God sent forth his Son, made of a woman, made under the law,
> To redeem them that were under the law, that we might receive the adoption of sons.
> And because ye are sons, God hath sent forth the Spirit of his Son into your hearts, crying, Abba, Father.
>
> Galatians 4:4-6

The Holy Spirit is the spirit of adoption that confirms within us that we are born again and new creatures, free from the bondage of sin. The book of I John was written that we may know we are born of God, and throughout the book, this freedom from sin is what John stresses as the evidence of the new birth. The Holy Spirit prompts us to hate sin, to love our brethren, to pray, to love God's Word, to fear God, and to live in holiness. And as we mature into these things, working out our salvation with fear and trembling,[236] He assures us of our salvation. This is not a feeling. It is a knowing. When the Spirit assures us of the adoption or new birth, we can boldly cry out, "Abba, Father," in full confidence that we are His. Those who lack this confidence should beware of a false hope. They may very well be a tare. Paris Reidhead concluded:

> No one in the universe has the right to tell a person he is born of God, except the Holy Spirit who is the Spirit of adoption.[237]

The lack of this witness by the Holy Spirit assuring the professing believer that he is one of God's children should be deeply troubling and indicative of someone who has never repented of their sins and been brought to true faith in Christ. They are headed for a potential tragedy on Judgment Day. John Wesley is quoted as having warned:

> So desperately wicked and so deceitful are the hearts of men that they flatter themselves by living in their sins until they come to their last breath. Thousands really believe they have found a way to live. But it is a broad way and will lead them to destruction.[238]

This false hope and false gospel has deceived millions, but it will not deceive God. The antinomian attack on repentance from sin has dethroned the law of God as holy and authoritative, and it has installed children of wrath in our pews. And it has not quashed the war against God that still rages within the hearts of these tares among wheat. Antinomianism has not disarmed the sinner and delivered him up to God waving a white flag. Instead, it has merely disarmed the gospel, ushering the sinner into the sheepfold through another door, and passing him off as one of the elect. Antinomianism is a device forged in the pit of hell and intended to bring about the fruits of peace without its surrender. But this false gospel will fail in the end. God is not mocked. The Bible says:

> Many will say to me in that day, Lord, Lord, have we not prophesied in thy name? and in thy name have cast out devils? and in thy name done many wonderful works?
> And then will I profess unto them, I never knew you: depart from me, ye that work iniquity.
>
> Matthew 7:22-23

On that day, those still clutching to the daggers of iniquity and harboring self-righteousness and revolt in their hearts will find that their church membership meant little to God. The salvation pronouncement of their pastor or peers was false. On that day, they will find no place of repentance, though they seek it carefully with tears. Every mouth will be stopped, and all the world will become guilty before God. And on that day, the tares will be separated out from the wheat, the changlings from the sons, the sinners from the saints. There will be weeping and gnashing of teeth. Their cheap, antinomian gospel will not stand the test of Judgment Day, and they will be forced to pay for their sins for all eternity.

But for those who flung down their weapons of warfare against God, repented of their sin, and ran out to God in full faith, they will find mercy. They will be judged by Christ's righteousness and not their own. They will sing the song of the redeemed, having been born not of blood nor of the will of the flesh, but of God. Through repentance toward God and faith toward our Lord Jesus Christ, God's children will be rewarded with a heavenly home and fellowship with the One who made them new. And on that day, the war will be ended.

The gospel will have won. Every knee will bow and every tongue confess that Jesus is Lord to the glory of God the Father.

AMEN.

Appendix A
"REPENT" MENTIONS IN THE BIBLE

Genesis 6:6
And it repented the LORD that he had made man on the earth, and it grieved him at his heart.

God turning from a past action He had done.

Exodus 13:17
And it came to pass, when Pharaoh had let the people go, that God led them not through the way of the land of the Philistines, although that was near; for God said, Lest peradventure the people repent when they see war, and they return to Egypt:

People turning from the action of traveling in a particular physical direction to go back in the opposite direction.

Exodus 32:12
Wherefore should the Egyptians speak, and say, For mischief did he bring them out, to slay them in the mountains, and to consume them from the face of the earth? Turn from thy fierce wrath, and repent of this evil against thy people.

God turning from a harmful action He intended.

Exodus 32:14
And the LORD repented of the evil which he thought to do unto his people.

God turning from a harmful action He intended.

Numbers 23:19
God is not a man, that he should lie; neither the son of man, that he should repent: hath he said, and shall he not do it? or hath he spoken, and shall he not make it good?

God hypothetically turning from an action He promised to do.

Deuteronomy 32:36
For the LORD shall judge his people, and repent himself for his servants, when he seeth that their power is gone, and there is none shut up, or left.

God feeling sorrow for, or sympathy with, someone.

Judges 2:18
And when the LORD raised them up judges, then the LORD was with the judge, and delivered them out of the hand of their enemies all the days of the judge: for it repented the LORD because of their groanings by reason of them that oppressed them and vexed them.

God feeling sorrow for someone's plight.

Judges 21:6
And the children of Israel repented them for Benjamin their brother, and said, There is one tribe cut off from Israel this day.

Israelites feeling sorrow for someone's plight.

Judges 21:15
And the people repented them for Benjamin, because that the LORD had made a breach in the tribes of Israel.

Israelites feeling sorrow for someone's plight.

I Samuel 15:11
It repenteth me that I have set up Saul to be king: for he is turned back from following me, and hath not performed my commandments. And it grieved Samuel; and he cried unto the LORD all night.

God regretting, or sorrowing over, an action He committed.

I Samuel 15:29
And also the Strength of Israel will not lie nor repent: for he is not a man, that he should repent.

God hypothetically turning from a direction or course of action intended.

I Samuel 15:35
And Samuel came no more to see Saul until the day of his death: nevertheless Samuel mourned for Saul: and the LORD repented that he had made Saul king over Israel.

God regretting, or sorrowing over, an action He committed.

II Samuel 24:16
And when the angel stretched out his hand upon Jerusalem to destroy it, the LORD repented him of the evil, and said to the angel that destroyed the people, It is enough: stay now thine hand. And the angel of the LORD was by the threshingplace of Araunah the Jebusite.

God turning from a harmful action He intended to do.

I Kings 8:47-48

Yet if they shall bethink themselves in the land whither they were carried captives, and repent, and make supplication unto thee in the land of them that carried them captives, saying, We have sinned, and have done perversely, we have committed wickedness;
And so return unto thee with all their heart, and with all their soul, in the land of their enemies, which led them away captive, and pray unto thee toward their land, which thou gavest unto their fathers, the city which thou hast chosen, and the house which I have built for thy name:

People turning from sin and turning to God.

I Chronicles 21:15

And God sent an angel unto Jerusalem to destroy it: and as he was destroying, the LORD beheld, and he repented him of the evil, and said to the angel that destroyed, It is enough, stay now thine hand. And the angel of the LORD stood by the threshingfloor of Ornan the Jebusite.

God turning from a harmful action He intended to do.

Job 42:6

Wherefore I abhor myself, and repent in dust and ashes.

Person regretting or turning from a sinful action committed against God (accusation).

Psalm 90:13

Return, O LORD, how long? and let it repent thee concerning thy servants.

God hypothetically having pity on, or sorrow for the plight of, His people.

Psalm 106:45
And he remembered for them his covenant, and repented according to the multitude of his mercies.

God having pity on His people and turning from actions committed against them (bringing them low – verse 44).

Psalm 110:4
The LORD hath sworn, and will not repent, Thou art a priest for ever after the order of Melchizedek.

God hypothetically turning from an action He intended to commit.

Psalm 135:14
For the LORD will judge his people, and he will repent himself concerning his servants.

God having sorrow or pity for the plight of His people.

Jeremiah 4:28
For this shall the earth mourn, and the heavens above be black; because I have spoken it, I have purposed it, and will not repent, neither will I turn back from it.

God hypothetically turning from a harmful action He intended to commit.

Jeremiah 8:6
I hearkened and heard, but they spake not aright: no man repented him of his wickedness, saying, What have I done? every one turned to his course, as the horse rusheth into the battle.

People hypothetically turning from sinful actions.

Jeremiah 15:6
Thou hast forsaken me, saith the LORD, thou art gone backward:

therefore will I stretch out my hand against thee, and destroy thee; I am weary with repenting.

God turning from harmful actions He intended to commit.

Jeremiah 18:8
If that nation, against whom I have pronounced, turn from their evil, I will repent of the evil that I thought to do unto them.

God turning from harmful actions He intended to commit.

Jeremiah 18:10
If it do evil in my sight, that it obey not my voice, then I will repent of the good, wherewith I said I would benefit them.

God turning from the good actions He intended to commit.

Jeremiah 20:16
And let that man be as the cities which the LORD overthrew, and repented not: and let him hear the cry in the morning, and the shouting at noontide;

God hypothetically turning from harmful actions He committed.

Jeremiah 26:3
If so be they will hearken, and turn every man from his evil way, that I may repent me of the evil, which I purpose to do unto them because of the evil of their doings.

God turning from the harmful actions He intended to commit.

Jeremiah 26:13
Therefore now amend your ways and your doings, and obey the voice of the LORD your God; and the LORD will repent him of the evil that he hath pronounced against you.

God turning from the harmful actions He intended to commit.

Jeremiah 26:19
Did Hezekiah king of Judah and all Judah put him at all to death? did he not fear the LORD, and besought the LORD, and the LORD repented him of the evil which he had pronounced against them? Thus might we procure great evil against our souls.

God turning from the harmful actions he intended to commit.

Jeremiah 31:19
Surely after that I was turned, I repented; and after that I was instructed, I smote upon my thigh: I was ashamed, yea, even confounded, because I did bear the reproach of my youth.

Ephraim being ashamed of, and turning from, sinful actions.

Jeremiah 42:10
If ye will still abide in this land, then will I build you, and not pull you down, and I will plant you, and not pluck you up: for I repent me of the evil that I have done unto you.

God turning away from the course of harmful actions He had been committing.

Ezekiel 14:6
Therefore say unto the house of Israel, Thus saith the Lord GOD; Repent, and turn yourselves from your idols; and turn away your faces from all your abominations.

Israel turning away from all their sins, especially the sinful action of idolatry.

Ezekiel 18:30
Therefore I will judge you, O house of Israel, every one according to his ways, saith the Lord GOD. Repent, and turn yourselves from all your transgressions; so iniquity shall not be your ruin.

People turning away from sinful actions.

Ezekiel 24:14

I the LORD have spoken it: it shall come to pass, and I will do it; I will not go back, neither will I spare, neither will I repent; according to thy ways, and according to thy doings, shall they judge thee, saith the Lord GOD.

God hypothetically turning from actions He said He would commit.

Hosea 11:8

How shall I give thee up, Ephraim? how shall I deliver thee, Israel? how shall I make thee as Admah? how shall I set thee as Zeboim? mine heart is turned within me, my repentings are kindled together.

God having pity on His people, and turning from actions committed and intended against them.

Hosea 13:14

I will ransom them from the power of the grave; I will redeem them from death: O death, I will be thy plagues; O grave, I will be thy destruction: repentance shall be hid from mine eyes.

God hypothetically turning from actions He intended.

Joel 2:13

And rend your heart, and not your garments, and turn unto the LORD your God: for he is gracious and merciful, slow to anger, and of great kindness, and repenteth him of the evil.

God turning from harmful actions He intended.

Joel 2:14

Who knoweth if he will return and repent, and leave a blessing behind him; even a meat offering and a drink offering unto the LORD your God?

God potentially turning from harmful actions He intended.

Amos 7:3
The LORD repented for this: It shall not be, saith the LORD.

God turning from harmful actions He intended.

Amos 7:6
The LORD repented for this: This also shall not be, saith the Lord GOD.

God turning from harmful actions He intended.

Jonah 3:9
Who can tell if God will turn and repent, and turn away from his fierce anger, that we perish not?

God turning from harmful actions He intended.

Jonah 3:10
And God saw their works, that they turned from their evil way; and God repented of the evil, that he had said that he would do unto them; and he did it not.

God turning from harmful actions He intended.

Jonah 4:2
And he prayed unto the LORD, and said, I pray thee, O LORD, was not this my saying, when I was yet in my country? Therefore I fled before unto Tarshish: for I knew that thou art a gracious God, and merciful, slow to anger, and of great kindness, and repentest thee of the evil.

God turning from harmful actions He intended.

Zechariah 8:14
For thus saith the LORD of hosts; As I thought to punish you, when

your fathers provoked me to wrath, saith the LORD of hosts, and I repented not:

God hypothetically turning from harmful actions He intended.

Matthew 3:2
And saying, Repent ye: for the kingdom of heaven is at hand.

People turning from sinful actions (verse 6).

Matthew 3:8
Bring forth therefore fruits meet for repentance:

Conversion, or people having turned from sinful actions (vs. 6).

Matthew 3:11
I indeed baptize you with water unto repentance. but he that cometh after me is mightier than I, whose shoes I am not worthy to bear: he shall baptize you with the Holy Ghost, and with fire:

People turning from sinful actions (verse 6).

Matthew 4:17
From that time Jesus began to preach, and to say, Repent: for the kingdom of heaven is at hand.

Passage not explicit.

Matthew 9:13
But go ye and learn what that meaneth, I will have mercy, and not sacrifice: for I am not come to call the righteous, but sinners to repentance.

Sin-sick sinners turning from their sinful actions unto the mercy of salvation.

Matthew 11:20
Then began he to upbraid the cities wherein most of his mighty
works were done, because they repented not.

Passage not explicit.

Matthew 11:21
Woe unto thee, Chorazin! woe unto thee, Bethsaida! for if the mighty
works, which were done in you, had been done in Tyre and Sidon,
they would have repented long ago in sackcloth and ashes.

Passage not explicit.

Matthew 12:41
The men of Nineveh shall rise in judgment with this generation, and
shall condemn it: because they repented at the preaching of Jonas;
and, behold, a greater than Jonas is here.

Sinners of Nineveh turning from their sinful actions.

Matthew 21:29
He answered and said, I will not: but afterward he repented, and
went.

Son turning from his sinful (disobedience) action intended.

Matthew 21:32
For John came unto you in the way of righteousness, and ye believed
him not: but the publicans and the harlots believed him: and ye,
when ye had seen it, repented not afterward, that ye might believe
him.

Sinners hypothetically turning from sinful actions (see context: vs.
29) to make room for belief.

Matthew 27:3
Then Judas, which had betrayed him, when he saw that he was

condemned, repented himself, and brought again the thirty pieces of silver to the chief priests and elders,

Sinner turning from his sinful action against Jesus and seeking to reverse the effects of his sin.

Mark 1:4
John did baptize in the wilderness, and preach the baptism of repentance for the remission of sins.

According to verse 5, the sinners repenting here were turning from or "confessing their sins."

Mark 1:15
And saying, The time is fulfilled, and the kingdom of God is at hand: repent ye, and believe the gospel.

One camp would say this refers to repentance making room for belief by removing sin, whereas the other might argue that this is simply defining repentance as belief; passage not explicit.

Mark 2:17
When Jesus heard it, he saith unto them, They that are whole have no need of the physician, but they that are sick: I came not to call the righteous, but sinners to repentance.

Sinners turning from sinful actions.

Mark 6:12
And they went out, and preached that men should repent.

Passage not explicit.

Luke 3:3
And he came into all the country about Jordan, preaching the baptism of repentance for the remission of sins.

People turning from sinful actions.

Luke 3:8
Bring forth therefore fruits worthy of repentance, and begin not to say within yourselves, We have Abraham to our father: for I say unto you, That God is able of these stones to raise up children unto Abraham.

A turn from sin that results in a change of actions, as opposed to a mere confession of being in the faith.

Luke 5:32
I came not to call the righteous, but sinners to repentance.

Sinners turning from their sinful actions.

Luke 10:13
Woe unto thee, Chorazin! woe unto thee, Bethsaida! for if the mighty works had been done in Tyre and Sidon, which have been done in you, they had a great while ago repented, sitting in sackcloth and ashes.

Passage not explicit.

Luke 11:32
The men of Nineve shall rise up in the judgment with this generation, and shall condemn it: for they repented at the preaching of Jonas; and, behold, a greater than Jonas is here.

People of Nineveh turning from their sinful actions.

Luke 13:3
I tell you, Nay: but, except ye repent, ye shall all likewise perish.

Sinners turning from sinful actions (see context in verse 2: "sinners").

Luke 13:5
I tell you, Nay: but, except ye repent, ye shall all likewise perish.

Sinners turning from sinful actions (see context in verse 4: "sinners").

Luke 15:7
I say unto you, that likewise joy shall be in heaven over one sinner that repenteth, more than over ninety and nine just persons, which need no repentance.

Sinners turning from sinful actions.

Luke 15:10
Likewise, I say unto you, there is joy in the presence of the angels of God over one sinner that repenteth.

Sinner turning from sinful actions.

Luke 16:30
And he said, Nay, father Abraham: but if one went unto them from the dead, they will repent.

People turning from unbelief to belief.

Luke 17:3
Take heed to yourselves: If thy brother trespass against thee, rebuke him; and if he repent, forgive him.

Brother turning from sinful actions against his brother.

Luke 17:4
And if he trespass against thee seven times in a day, and seven times in a day turn again to thee, saying, I repent; thou shalt forgive him.

Brother turning from sinful actions against his brother.

Luke 24:47
And that repentance and remission of sins should be preached in his name among all nations, beginning at Jerusalem.

People turning from sinful actions.

Acts 2:38
Then Peter said unto them, Repent, and be baptized every one of you in the name of Jesus Christ for the remission of sins, and ye shall receive the gift of the Holy Ghost.

People turning from sins.

Acts 3:19
Repent ye therefore, and be converted, that your sins may be blotted out, when the times of refreshing shall come from the presence of the Lord.

People turning from sins.

Acts 5:31
Him hath God exalted with his right hand to be a Prince and a Saviour, for to give repentance to Israel, and forgiveness of sins.

People turning from sins.

Acts 8:22
Repent therefore of this thy wickedness, and pray God, if perhaps the thought of thine heart may be forgiven thee.

Person hypothetically turning from wicked actions intended.

Acts 11:18
When they heard these things, they held their peace, and glorified

God, saying, Then hath God also to the Gentiles granted repentance unto life.

Passage not explicit.

Acts 13:24
When John had first preached before his coming the baptism of repentance to all the people of Israel.

People turning from sins (see Matthew 3:6).

Acts 17:30
And the times of this ignorance God winked at; but now commandeth all men every where to repent:

People turning from the sin of idolatry.

Acts 19:4
Then said Paul, John verily baptized with the baptism of repentance, saying unto the people, that they should believe on him which should come after him, that is, on Christ Jesus.

People turning from sins (see Matthew 3:6).

Acts 20:21
Testifying both to the Jews, and also to the Greeks, repentance toward God, and faith toward our Lord Jesus Christ.

Passage not explicit.

Acts 26:20
But shewed first unto them of Damascus, and at Jerusalem, and throughout all the coasts of Judaea, and then to the Gentiles, that they should repent and turn to God, and do works meet for repentance.

People turning from sin (verse 18), from darkness to light, resulting in a change of actions.

Romans 2:4

Or despisest thou the riches of his goodness and forbearance and longsuffering; not knowing that the goodness of God leadeth thee to repentance?

A turning away from sinful actions listed earlier in the chapter.

Romans 11:29

For the gifts and calling of God are without repentance.

God hypothetically turning from the action of calling Israel.

II Corinthians 7:8

For though I made you sorry with a letter, I do not repent, though I did repent: for I perceive that the same epistle hath made you sorry, though it were but for a season.

Regret for the action of sending a letter.

II Corinthians 7:9-10

Now I rejoice, not that ye were made sorry, but that ye sorrowed to repentance: for ye were made sorry after a godly manner, that ye might receive damage by us in nothing.
For godly sorrow worketh repentance to salvation not to be repented of: but the sorrow of the world worketh death.

Regret for sin that extends beyond mere sorrow of mind to salvation and change of action.

II Corinthians 12:21

And lest, when I come again, my God will humble me among you, and that I shall bewail many which have sinned already, and have not repented of the uncleanness and fornication and lasciviousness which they have committed.

Sinners turning from sins.

II Timothy 2:25
In meekness instructing those that oppose themselves; if God peradventure will give them repentance to the acknowledging of the truth;

Turning to the truth from a lie.

Hebrews 6:1
Therefore leaving the principles of the doctrine of Christ, let us go on unto perfection; not laying again the foundation of repentance from dead works, and of faith toward God,

Turning from actions that bring death.

Hebrews 6:6
If they shall fall away, to renew them again unto repentance; seeing they crucify to themselves the Son of God afresh, and put him to an open shame.

A general reference to salvation. Not explicit.

Hebrews 7:21
(For those priests were made without an oath; but this with an oath by him that said unto him, The Lord sware and will not repent, Thou art a priest for ever after the order of Melchisedec:)

God hypothetically reversing an action He committed.

Hebrews 12:17
For ye know how that afterward, when he would have inherited

the blessing, he was rejected: for he found no place of repentance,
though he sought it carefully with tears.

Reversing an action committed.

II Peter 3:9
The Lord is not slack concerning his promise, as some men count
slackness; but is longsuffering to us-ward, not willing that any
should perish, but that all should come to repentance.

Passage not explicit.

Revelation 2:5
Remember therefore from whence thou art fallen, and repent, and do
the first works; or else I will come unto thee quickly, and will remove
thy candlestick out of his place, except thou repent.

Christians returning to good works or actions.

Revelation 2:16
Repent; or else I will come unto thee quickly, and will fight against
them with the sword of my mouth.

Turning from the sinful action of harboring heretics.

Revelation 2:21-22
And I gave her space to repent of her fornication; and she repented
not.
Behold, I will cast her into a bed, and them that commit adultery
with her into great tribulation, except they repent of their deeds.

Turning from sinful acts committed.

Revelation 3:3
Remember therefore how thou hast received and heard, and hold
fast, and repent. If therefore thou shalt not watch, I will come on

thee as a thief, and thou shalt not know what hour I will come upon thee.

Turning from sinful actions committed.

Revelation 3:19
As many as I love, I rebuke and chasten: be zealous therefore, and repent.

Turning from sins, including the sin of lukewarmness.

Revelation 9:20-21
And the rest of the men which were not killed by these plagues yet repented not of the works of their hands, that they should not worship devils, and idols of gold, and silver, and brass, and stone, and of wood: which neither can see, nor hear, nor walk: Neither repented they of their murders, nor of their sorceries, nor of their fornication, nor of their thefts.

Hypothetically turning from sinful works or actions committed.

Revelation 16:9
And men were scorched with great heat, and blasphemed the name of God, which hath power over these plagues: and they repented not to give him glory.

Turning from sinful ways.

Revelation 16:11
And blasphemed the God of heaven because of their pains and their sores, and repented not of their deeds.

Turning from sinful actions.

Appendix B

THE SCRIPTURAL
SYLLOGISM

Chapters 4, 5, and 6 present a logical syllogism from the Bible. Chapter 4 demonstrates that repentance, regardless of how it is defined, is a biblical requirement for salvation. Chapter 5 defines the term, *repentance*, as a turn or change of heart and mind from an action, committed or intended, resulting in a change of course – and in the context of humanity and the gospel, that action is almost always sin. Chapter 6 concludes from these two premises that the gospel requires a turn from sin. Below, this syllogism is reduced to only the scriptures supporting each statement.

Premise 1: The gospel requires "repentance," regardless of how it is defined.

Matthew 3:1-10
In those days came John the Baptist, preaching in the wilderness of Judaea,
And saying, Repent ye: for the kingdom of heaven is at hand.
For this is he that was spoken of by the prophet Esaias, saying, The voice of one crying in the wilderness, Prepare ye the way of the Lord, make his paths straight.
And the same John had his raiment of camel's hair, and a leathern girdle about his loins; and his meat was locusts and wild honey.
Then went out to him Jerusalem, and all Judaea, and all the region round about Jordan,

And were baptized of him in Jordan, confessing their sins.

But when he saw many of the Pharisees and Sadducees come to his baptism, he said unto them, O generation of vipers, who hath warned you to flee from the wrath to come?

Bring forth therefore fruits meet for repentance:

And think not to say within yourselves, We have Abraham to our father: for I say unto you, that God is able of these stones to raise up children unto Abraham.

And now also the axe is laid unto the root of the trees: therefore every tree which bringeth not forth good fruit is hewn down, and cast into the fire.

Matthew 4:17

From that time Jesus began to preach, and to say, Repent: for the kingdom of heaven is at hand.

Matthew 9:13

But go ye and learn what that meaneth, I will have mercy, and not sacrifice: for I am not come to call the righteous, but sinners to repentance.

Mark 1:15

And saying, The time is fulfilled, and the kingdom of God is at hand: repent ye, and believe the gospel.

Mark 6:12

And they went out, and preached that men should repent.

Luke 13:2-5

And Jesus answering said unto them, Suppose ye that these Galilaeans were sinners above all the Galilaeans, because they suffered such things?

I tell you, Nay: but, except ye repent, ye shall all likewise perish. Or those eighteen, upon whom the tower in Siloam fell, and slew them, think ye that they were sinners above all men that dwelt in Jerusalem?

I tell you, Nay: but, except ye repent, ye shall all likewise perish.

Luke 15: 7, 10
I say unto you, that likewise joy shall be in heaven over one sinner that repenteth, more than over ninety and nine just persons, which need no repentance.
Likewise, I say unto you, there is joy in the presence of the angels of God over one sinner that repenteth.

Luke 24:46-48
And said unto them, Thus it is written, and thus it behooved Christ to suffer, and to rise from the dead the third day:
And that repentance and remission of sins should be preached in his name among all nations, beginning at Jerusalem.
And ye are witnesses of these things.

Acts 2:38
Then Peter said unto them, Repent, and be baptized every one of you in the name of Jesus Christ for the remission of sins, and ye shall receive the gift of the Holy Ghost.

Acts 3:19
Repent ye therefore, and be converted, that your sins may be blotted out, when the times of refreshing shall come from the presence of the Lord.

Acts 17:30
And the times of this ignorance God winked at; but now commandeth all men every where to repent:

Acts 20:21
Testifying both to the Jews, and also to the Greeks, repentance toward God, and faith toward our Lord Jesus Christ.

II Corinthians 7:10
Testifying both to the Jews, and also to the Greeks, repentance toward God, and faith toward our Lord Jesus Christ.

Premise 2: When in the context of mankind, repentance almost always means a turn or change of heart and mind from sin.

Ezekiel 14:6
Therefore say unto the house of Israel, Thus saith the Lord God; Repent, and turn yourselves from your idols; and turn away your faces from all your abominations.

Ezekiel 18:30-32
Therefore I will judge you, O house of Israel, every one according to his ways, saith the Lord God. Repent, and turn yourselves from all your transgressions; so iniquity shall not be your ruin.
Cast away from you all your transgressions, whereby ye have transgressed; and make you a new heart and a new spirit: for why will ye die, O house of Israel?
For I have no pleasure in the death of him that dieth, saith the Lord God: wherefore turn yourselves, and live ye.

Luke 17:3
Take heed to yourselves: If thy brother trespass against thee, rebuke him; and if he repent, forgive him.

Acts 3:19, 26
Repent ye therefore, and be converted, that your sins may be blotted out, when the times of refreshing shall come from the presence of the Lord.
Unto you first God, having raised up his Son Jesus, sent him to bless you, in turning away every one of you from his iniquities.

Acts 8:22-23
Repent therefore of this thy wickedness, and pray God, if perhaps the thought of thine heart may be forgiven thee.
For I perceive that thou art in the gall of bitterness, and in the bond of iniquity.

II Corinthians 7:10
Testifying both to the Jews, and also to the Greeks, repentance toward God, and faith toward our Lord Jesus Christ.

II Corinthians 12:21
And lest, when I come again, my God will humble me among you, and that I shall bewail many which have sinned already, and have not repented of the uncleanness and fornication and lasciviousness which they have committed.

Revelation 2:21-22
And I gave her space to repent of her fornication; and she repented not.
Behold, I will cast her into a bed, and them that commit adultery with her into great tribulation, except they repent of their deeds.

Revelation 9:20-21
And the rest of the men which were not killed by these plagues yet repented not of the works of their hands, that they should not worship devils, and idols of gold, and silver, and brass, and stone, and of wood: which neither can see, nor hear, nor walk:
Neither repented they of their murders, nor of their sorceries, nor of their fornication, nor of their thefts.

Revelation 16:11
And blasphemed the God of heaven because of their pains and their sores, and repented not of their deeds.

Conclusion: Ergo, the gospel requires a turn from sin.

Isaiah 55:6-7
Seek ye the Lord while he may be found, call ye upon him while he is near:
Let the wicked forsake his way, and the unrighteous man his thoughts: and let him return unto the Lord, and he will have mercy upon him; and to our God, for he will abundantly pardon.

Matthew 3:1-10

In those days came John the Baptist, preaching in the wilderness of Judaea,

And saying, Repent ye: for the kingdom of heaven is at hand.

For this is he that was spoken of by the prophet Esaias, saying, The voice of one crying in the wilderness, Prepare ye the way of the Lord, make his paths straight.

And the same John had his raiment of camel's hair, and a leathern girdle about his loins; and his meat was locusts and wild honey.

Then went out to him Jerusalem, and all Judaea, and all the region round about Jordan,

And were baptized of him in Jordan, confessing their sins.

But when he saw many of the Pharisees and Sadducees come to his baptism, he said unto them, O generation of vipers, who hath warned you to flee from the wrath to come?

Bring forth therefore fruits meet for repentance:

And think not to say within yourselves, We have Abraham to our father: for I say unto you, that God is able of these stones to raise up children unto Abraham.

And now also the axe is laid unto the root of the trees: therefore every tree which bringeth not forth good fruit is hewn down, and cast into the fire.

Acts 3:19, 26

Repent ye therefore, and be converted, that your sins may be blotted out, when the times of refreshing shall come from the presence of the Lord.

Unto you first God, having raised up his Son Jesus, sent him to bless you, in turning away every one of you from his iniquities.

Acts 11:21

And the hand of the Lord was with them: and a great number believed, and turned unto the Lord.

Acts 14:15

And saying, Sirs, why do ye these things? We also are men of like passions with you, and preach unto you that ye should turn from these vanities unto the living God, which made heaven, and earth, and the sea, and all things that are therein:

Acts 26:18
To open their eyes, and to turn them from darkness to light, and from the power of Satan unto God, that they may receive forgiveness of sins, and inheritance among them which are sanctified by faith that is in me.

II Corinthians 7:10
Testifying both to the Jews, and also to the Greeks, repentance toward God, and faith toward our Lord Jesus Christ.

I Thessalonians 1:9
For they themselves shew of us what manner of entering in we had unto you, and how ye turned to God from idols to serve the living and true God;

Hebrews 6:1
Therefore leaving the principles of the doctrine of Christ, let us go on unto perfection; not laying again the foundation of repentance from dead works, and of faith toward God,

James 5:20
Let him know, that he which converteth the sinner from the error of his way shall save a soul from death, and shall hide a multitude of sins.

NOTES

1. Bunyan, p. 107.
2. *Holy Bible*, Matthew 7:13-14.
3. Ibid., Matthew 13:28.
4. Ibid., Romans 8:19.
5. Ibid., I John 2:19.
6. Luther, *Decalogue*, p. 33.
7. Reidhead, "Ten Shekels and a Shirt."
8. Ibid.
9. Hyles, *Enemies of Soul Winning*, pp. 38-39.
10. Champion, "Dr. Jack Hyles."
11. Cloud, *The Hyles Effect*, pp. 53-69.
12. *Holy Bible*, Mark 10:25.
13. Ibid., Matthew 11:30.
14. Ibid., Acts 20:21.
15. Ibid., Luke 13:3, 5.
16. Ibid., II Corinthians 7:10.
17. Ibid., Acts 3:19.
18. Ibid., Ezekiel 13:31.
19. Ibid., Luke 24:47.
20. Monck, *Orthodox Baptist Creed*, Article XII, p. 156.
21. Baptist Association, *Philadelphia Baptist Confession of Faith*, p. 42.
22. Brown, *New Hampshire Confession of Faith*, Article VIII.
23. Nowlin, *Fundamentals of the Faith*.
24. Webster, s.v. "Repent, v. i."
25. Ibid., s.v. "Repentance, n."
26. Ibid., s.v. "Turn, v. t." and s.v. "Turn, v. i."

27. Turner, p. 2.

28. Ibid.

29. Ibid., p. 6.

30. *Holy Bible*, Psalm 19:7.

31. Reidhead, *Finding the Reality of God*, p. 54.

32. Reidhead, "Ten Shekels and a Shirt."

33. Henry, vol. 4, p. 647.

34. *Holy Bible*, Hebrews 12:14.

35. Correspondence on file with the author.

36. Ibid.

37. Ibid.

38. Jacobs, p. 18.

39. Richard, p. 379.

40. Melancthon, Article XII.

41. Jacobs, p. 18.

42. MacKinnon, p. 162.

43. Ibid., p. 164.

44. Luther, *Decalogue*, p. 12.

45. MacKinnon, pp. 171-172.

46. *Holy Bible*, Matthew 19:24.

47. Luther, "Against the Antinomians."

48. Luther, *Decalogue*, pp. 12-14.

49. Ibid., p. 14.

50. Jacobs, p. 18.

51. MacKinnon, pp. 173-174.

52. Ibid., p. 175.

53. Ibid., p. 176.

54. Brecht, p. 169.

55. Ibid., p. 170.

56. Ibid.

57. Luther, "Against the Antinomians."

58. Jacobs, p. 18.

59. Cloud, *Repentance and Soul-Winning*, p. 82.

60. Ibid., p. 84.

61. Luther, *Decalogue*, p. 26.

62. Cloud, "Carl Hatch Squeeze."

63. Ellis, "3 Reasons."

64. Luther, *Decalogue*, p. 24.

65. Luther, "Against the Antinomians."

66. Anderson, *RepentanceBlacklist.com*.

67. Anderson, *Repent of Your Sins Heresy*.

68. Ibid.

69. Ibid.

70. *Holy Bible*, Ephesians 5:5-6.

71. Ibid., Romans 7:7-13.

72. Luther, *Decalogue*, p. 24.

73. Green, "A Review Article."

74. Boyd, *Repentance From Sin*.

75. Luther, *Decalogue*, p. 76.

76. Hyles, *Enemies of Soul Winning*, p. 3.

77. Ibid., p. 34.

78. Luther, *Decalogue*, p. 12.

79. Hyles, *Enemies of Soul Winning*, p. 31.

80. Ibid., p. 33.

81. Ibid., p. 35.

82. Ibid., p. 39.

83. Luther, *Decalogue*, p. 26.

84. Ibid., p. 51.

85. Ibid., p. 81.

86. *Holy Bible*, I Peter 2:5.

87. Ibid., Hebrews 11:1.

88. Ibid., Hebrews 12:1.

89. Ibid., II Peter 3:15.

90. Ibid., II Timothy 2:2.

91. Tertullian, "On Repentance."

92. Ibid.

93. Cloud, *Repentance and Soul-Winning*, p. 21.

94. Ibid., p. 81.

95.   Backus, p. 45.

96.   Ibid., pp. 21-22.

97.   Ibid., pp. 22-23.

98.   Spurgeon, "The Royal Savior," pp. 4-5.

99.   Thornton, p. 152.

100. Cloud, *Way of Life Encyclopedia*, p. 524.

101. Ibid.

102. Monck, *Orthodox Baptist Creed*, Article XII, p. 156.

103. Brown, *New Hampshire Confession of Faith*, Article VIII.

104. Nowlin, *Fundamentals of the Faith*.

105. Thornton, p. 150.

106. Cloud, *Repentance and Soul-Winning*, p. 27.

107. Ibid., p. 30.

108. Ibid., pp. 28-29.

109. Ibid., p. 32.

110. Canton Baptist Temple, "George Beauchamp Vick."

111. Cloud, *Repentance and Soul-Winning*, p. 32.

112. Rice, "What Must I Do?"

113. Cloud, *Repentance and Soul-Winning*, p. 33.

114. Ibid.

115. Thornton, p. 150.

116. Greene, *TheGospelHour.org*.

117. Cloud, *Repentance and Soul-Winning*, p. 33.

118. Cloud, "Bruce Lackey."

119. Cloud, *Repentance and Soul-Winning*, p. 35.

120. Reese, "Lester Roloff."

121. Roloff, *Repent or Perish*.

122. Ibid.

123. Dearing, Part 1.

124. Ibid.

125. Canton Baptist Temple, "Henry A. Ironside."

126. Ironside, p. 172.

127. Tyndale Theological Seminary, "J. Dwight Pentecost."

128. Cloud, *Repentance and Soul-Winning*, p. 49.

129. *Holy Bible*, Matthew 1:21.

130. Ibid., Luke 17:3-4.

131. Ironside, pp. 51-52.

132. *Holy Bible*, Job 33:14.

133. Ibid., Mark 6:12.

134. Ibid., Matthew 3:6.

135. Henry, vol. 1, pp. 362-363.

136. *Holy Bible*, I Corinthians 2:13.

137. Henry, vol. 6, p. 268.

138. Backus, p. 255.

139. Cloud, *Repentance and Soul-Winning*, p. 46.

140. *Holy Bible*, Isaiah 64:6.

141. Ibid., Job 42:5-6.

142. Reidhead, "Ten Shekels and a Shirt."

143. Ironside, p. 159.

144. *Holy Bible*, Exodus 9:27.

145. Ibid., I Kings 8:33.

146. Henry, vol. 2, p. 482.

147. Ruckman, *Peter Ruckman On Repentance*.

148. *Holy Bible*, Matthew 3:8.

149. Cloud, *Repentance and Soul-Winning*, p. 81.

150. *Holy Bible*, Matthew 3:6.

151. Ibid., Proverbs 28:13.

152. Bunyan, p. 53.

153. Ironside, p. 74.

154. Cloud, *Repentance and Soul-Winning*, p. 74.

155. *Holy Bible*, Matthew 3:8.

156. Reidhead, *Finding the Reality of God*, p. 92.

157. Ibid., pp. 32-33.

158. *Holy Bible*, I Thessalonians 1:9.

159. Ibid., Romans 6:23.

160. Ibid., Romans 10:13.

161. Ibid., Matthew 25:46.

162. Ibid., I Corinthians 6:9.

163. Ibid., Romans 7:9.

164. Ibid., John 3:18.

165. Ibid. James 2:19.

166. Ibid., Matthew 8:29.

167. Ibid., Acts 8:37.

168. Ibid., James 2:20.

169. Ibid., Psalm 66:18.

170. Ironside, pp. 9-11.

171. Bunyan, p. 93.

172. *Holy Bible*, Matthew 13:46.

173. Ibid., Psalm 66:18.

174. Ibid., II Kings 7:3-8.

175. Ibid., John 6:35.

176. Cloud, *Repentance and Soul-Winning*, p. 3.

177. Webster, s.v. "Turn, v. i."

178. *Holy Bible*, Matthew 9:13.

179. Reidhead, *Finding the Reality of God*, p. 82.

180. Hyles, *On Justice*, p. 87.

181. Hyles, *Enemies of Soul Winning*, pp. 29-31.

182. *Holy Bible*, Romans 5:12.

183. Ibid., Revelation 20:6.

184. Ibid., Romans 6:23.

185. Hyles, *Enemies of Soul Winning*, p. 30.

186. *Holy Bible*, Acts 20:21.

187. Ibid., Romans 2:12.

188. Anderson, *Repent of Your Sins Heresy*.

189. *Holy Bible*, John 1:9.

190. Ravenhill, "What Have You Been Saved From?"

191. *Holy Bible*, Galatians 2:20.

192. Ibid., Romans 6:11.

193. Henry, vol. 5, p. 494.

194. Henry, vol. 4, p. 198.

195. Ironside, p. 76.

196. *Holy Bible*, Habakkuk 1:13.

197. Whitefield, p. 370.
198. *Holy Bible*, Romans 8:29.
199. Ibid., Psalm 96:9.
200. Wesley, p. 93.
201. Whitefield, pp. 323-324.
202. Hyles, "Worthy Is the Lamb."
203. *Holy Bible*, Philippians 2:11.
204. Ibid., I John 3:4-8.
205. Cloud, *Repentance and Soul-Winning*, p. 74.
206. *Holy Bible*, Mark 10:21.
207. Ibid., Numbers 23:19 and Romans 11:29.
208. Ibid., Acts 8:21.
209. Ibid., Acts 8:24.
210. Reidhead, *Finding the Reality of God*, pp. 86-87.
211. Ironside, pp. 52-53.
212. *Holy Bible*, II Timothy 3:16.
213. Spurgeon, "The Bible," par. 7.
214. *Holy Bible*, Ephesians 2:8.
215. Ibid., Matthew 3:8.
216. Luther, *Decalogue*, p. 50.
217. Ironside, pp. 10-11.
218. *Holy Bible*, Matthew 5:28.
219. Ibid., I John 3:15.
220. Ibid., Genesis 15:6.
221. Reidhead, *Finding the Reality of God*, p. 46.
222. *Holy Bible*, Galatians 1:15-16.
223. Ibid., Mark 10:21.
224. Reidhead, *Finding the Reality of God*, p. 19.
225. *Holy Bible*, Romans 3:20.
226. Edwards, p. 15.
227. Luther, *Decalogue*, p. 86.
228. Henry, vol. 5, p. 17.
229. *Holy Bible*, Genesis 42:21.
230. Reidhead, *Finding the Reality of God*, p. 117.

231. *Holy Bible*, John 14:6.

232. Ibid., James 2:24.

233. Henry, vol. 6, p. 790.

234. *Holy Bible*, I John 3:8, 10.

235. Ibid., Titus 2:14.

236. Ibid., Philippians 2:12.

237. Reidhead, *Finding the Reality of God*, p. 116.

238. Ibid., p. 117.

BIBLIOGRAPHY

Anderson, Steven. 2016. *Repent of Your Sins Heresy*. 1:06:19. YouTube video. Channel: StephenKJV1611. Accessed January 13, 2017. https://www.youtube.com/watch?v=AOkJyOcxkaQ.

—. n.d. *RepentanceBlacklist.com*. Accessed January 13, 2017. http://repentanceblacklist.com/.

Backus, Isaac. 1804. *An Abridgment of the Church History of New-England from 1602 to 1804*. Boston: E. Lincoln. http://bit.ly/2imsZA5.

Baptist Association at Philadelphia. 1742. *Philadelphia Baptist Confession of Faith*. Tri-Centennial Edition (2007 reprint). Asheville, NC: Revival Literature.

Boyd, Dr. Don. 2010. *Repentance From Sin for Salvation Not in the Bible*. 3:28. YouTube video. Channel: mindquest1. https://www.youtube.com/watch?v=2V_MYL836iw.

Brecht, Martin. 1987. *Martin Luther: the Preservation of the Church 1532-1546*. Paperback (1999). Translated by James L. Schaaf. Minneapolis, MN: Fortress Press.

Brown, J. Newton. 1833. *The New Hampshire Confession of Faith*. Digitized (2007). BaptistStudiesOnline.com. Accessed January 14, 2017. http://bit.ly/2kc8EOx.

Bunyan, John. 1914. *Pilgrim's Progress and Holy War*. New York: The Walter Scott Publishing Co.

Canton Baptist Temple. n.d. "George Beauchamp Vick." *Christian Hall of Fame* (website). Accessed January 13, 2017. http://christianhof.org/vick/.

—. n.d. "Henry A. Ironside." *Christian Hall of Fame* (website). Accessed January 14, 2017. http://christianhof.org/ironside/.

Champion, Dr. HL. 2011. "Dr. Jack Hyles." *Baptist.org*. Accessed January 14, 2017. http://www.baptist.org/dr-jack-hyles/.

Cloud, David W. 2016. "Repentance." In *Way of Life Encyclopedia of the Bible & Christianity*, edited by David W. Cloud. Port Huron, MI: Way of Life Literature.

—. 2000. *Repentance and Soul-Winning*. Fifth Edition. Port Huron, MI: Way of Life Literature.

—. 2004. "Testimonies of KJV Defenders - Bruce Lackey." *WayOfLife.org*. Accessed January 13, 2017. http://www.wayoflife.org/database/lackey.html.

—. 2014. *The Hyles Effect: A Spreading Blight*. Fourth Edition. Port Huron, MI: Way of Life Literature.

—. 2016. "The Sword of the Lord and the Carl Hatch Squeeze." *WayOfLife.org*. Accessed January 13, 2017. http://www.wayoflife.org/reports/sword_of_lord_and_carl_hatch.html.

Dearing, Joseph. 2013. *What Is Repentance?* Kindle Edition. DayStar Publishing.

Edwards, Jonathan. 1741. "Sinners in the Hands of an Angry God." *Electronic Texts in American Studies. Paper 54.* Edited by Reiner Smolinski. Accessed January 14, 2017. http://bit.ly/2ioW1iG.

Ellis, Paul. 2011. "3 Reasons Why I Don't Preach on Repentance ('Turn from Sin')." *EscapeToReality.org*. Accessed January 13, 2017. https://escapetoreality.org/2011/11/28/3-reasons-why-i-dont-preach-on-repentance/.

Green, Lowell C. 2000. "A Review Article: Law and Gospel: Philip Melanchthon's Debate with John Agricola of Eisleben over 'Poenitentia'." *Concordia Theological Quarterly* 64:1. http://www.ctsfw.net/media/pdfs/greenlawgospeldebate.pdf.

Greene, Oliver B. 2017. *TheGospelHour.org*. Accessed January 13, 2017. http://www.thegospelhour.org/.

Henry, Matthew. 1991. *Matthew Henry's Commentary on the Whole Bible*. New Modern Edition, Complete and Unabridged. Vol. 1. 6 vols. Peabody, MA: Hendrickson Publishers.

—. Vol. 2.

—. Vol. 4.

—. Vol. 5.

—. Vol. 6.

Hyles, Jack. 1993. *Enemies of Soul Winning.* Hammond, IN: Hyles-Anderson Publishers.

—. 1992. *On Justice.* Hammond, IN: Hyles-Anderson Publishers.

—. 2017. "Worthy is the Lamb." *JackHyles.us.* Accessed January 14, 2017. http://jackhyles.us/?p=201.

Ironside, Harry A. 1937. *Except Ye Repent.* Grand Rapids, MI: Baker Book House.

Jacobs, John Augustus William Hass and Henry Eyster, ed. 1899. *The Lutheran Cyclopedia.* Digitized (2008). New York: Scribner.

Luther, Martin. 1539. "Against the Antinomians." In *Luther's Works, Vol. 47, The Christian in Society IV,* edited by Franklin Sherman and Helmut Lehmann, translated by Martin Bertram. Republished (1971). Philadelphia: Fortress Press.

—. 2008. *Only the Decalogue is Eternal: Martin Luther's Complete Antinomian Theses and Disputations.* Edited by Holger Sonntag. Translated by Holger Sonntag. Minneapolis, MN: Lutheran Press.

MacKinnon, John. 1962. *Luther and the Reformation IV: Vindication of the Movement.* 4 vols. New York: Russell & Russell, Inc.

Melancthon et al., Philipp. 1530. *The Unaltered Augsburg Confession.* Republished (2005). Translated by Glen L. Thompson. Milwaukee, WI: Northwestern Publishing House. Accessed January 13, 2017. http://bit.ly/2jyQbZg.

Monck et al., Thomas. 1679. "An Orthodox Baptist Creed." *Southwestern Journal of Theology* (Southwestern Baptist Theological Seminary) 48:2. Accessed January 14, 2017. http://www.baptisttheology.org/baptisttheology/assets/File/OrthodoxCreed.pdf.

Nowlin, William D. 1922. "Chapter VI: Regeneration." In *Fundamentals of the Faith*, by William D. Nowlin. Accessed January 14, 2017. http://spbaptists.info/articles/fundamentals06.html.

Ravenhill, Leonard. 2010. "What Have You Been Saved From?" *Leonard-Ravenhill.com*. Accessed January 14, 2017. http://www.leonard-ravenhill.com/what-have-you-been-saved-from/213.html.

Reese, Edward. n.d. "Lester Roloff." *EarnestlyContending.com*. Accessed January 13, 2017. http://www.earnestlycontending.com/KT/bios/lesterroloff.html.

Reidhead, Paris. 1989. *Finding the Reality of God*. Denton, MD: Bible Teaching Ministries, Inc.

—. n.d. "Ten Shekels and a Shirt." *Paris Reidhead Bible Teaching Ministries*. Accessed January 7, 2017. http://www.parisreidheadbibleteachingministries.org/pdf/tenshekels.pdf.

Rice, John R. n.d. "What Must I Do to Be Saved?" *WholesomeWords.org*. Accessed January 13, 2017. http://www.wholesomewords.org/resources/saved.html.

Richard, James William. 1898. *Philip Melanchthon, the Protestant Preceptor of Germany*. New York and London: G.P. Putnam's Sons.

Roloff, Lester. 2011. *Repent or Perish*. 45:17. YouTube video. Channel: Aaron G. Accessed January 13, 2017. https://www.youtube.com/watch?v=DJIjGUmFnKU.

Ruckman, Peter S. n.d. *Peter Ruckman On Repentance*. 1:35. YouTube video. Channel: Nicholas Murphy. Accessed January 13, 2017. https://www.youtube.com/watch?v=Ytn5KUSibtg.

Spurgeon, Charles. 1855. "The Bible." *WhatSaithTheScripture.com*. Accessed January 14, 2017. http://bit.ly/2jKmm6L.

—. 1872. "The Royal Savior." *SpurgeonGems.org*. Accessed January 13, 2017. http://www.spurgeongems.org/vols55-57/chs3229.pdf.

Tertullian. n.d. "On Repentance." *Tertullian.org.* Translated by Rev. S. Thelwall. Accessed January 13, 2017. http://www.tertullian.org/anf/anf03/anf03-47.htm.

Thornton, J. 1834. *Repentance.* Republished (2011). Milton, FL: Victory Baptist Press.

Turner, Dr. David. n.d. *The Turn.* Ashville, AL: Gulf Coast Prison Ministries.

Tyndale Theological Seminary. n.d. "J. Dwight Pentecost." *Tyndale.edu.* Accessed January 19, 2017. http://bit.ly/2k6wXsT.

Webster, Noah. 1828. *American Dictionary of the English Language.* Facsimile Reprint (2006). Chesapeake, VA: Foundation for American Christian Association.

Wesley, Charles. 1968. "Hark! the Herald Angels Sing." In *Great Hymns of the Faith*, edited by John W. Peterson. Franklin, TN: Brentwood-Benson Music Publishing, Inc.

Whitefield, George. 1960. *Whitefield's Journals.* Edited by Iain Murray. London: The Banner of Truth Trust.

SCRIPTURE INDEX